complete
basements
attics & bonus rooms

plan & build your dream space

Better Homes and Gardens® Books
Des Moines, Iowa

Better Homes and Gardens® Books
An imprint of Meredith® Books

Complete Basements, Attics & Bonus Rooms
Editor: Brian Kramer
Project Editors and Writesr: Cynthia Pearson, Dan Weeks
Art Director: Mick Schnepf
Contributing Art Director: Brad Ruppert, Studio G
Copy Chief: Terri Fredrickson
Copy and Production Editor: Victoria Forlini
Editorial Operations Manager: Karen Schirm
Managers, Book Production: Pam Kvitne, Marjorie J. Schenkelberg
Contributing Copy Editor: Kim Catanzarite
Contributing Proofreaders: Ellen Bingham, Sue Fetters, Willa Speiser
Contributing Photographers: n-haus photography
Contributing Illustrator: TheArt Factory
Indexer: Kathleen Poole
Electronic Production Coordinator: Paula Forest
Editorial and Design Assistants: Kaye Chabot, Karen McFadden, Mary Lee Gavin

Meredith® Books
Publisher and Editor in Chief: James D. Blume
Design Director: Matt Strelecki
Managing Editor: Gregory H. Kayko
Executive Editor, Home Decorating and Design: Denise L. Caringer

Director, Operations: George A. Susral
Director, Production: Douglas M. Johnston
Executive Director, Sales: Ken Zagor

Vice President and General Manager: Douglas J. Guendel

Better Homes and Gardens® Magazine
Editor in Chief: Karol DeWulf Nickell

Meredith Publishing Group
President, Publishing Group: Stephen M. Lacy
Vice President-Publishing Director: Bob Mate

Meredith Corporation
Chairman and Chief Executive Officer: William T. Kerr

Chairman of the Executive Committee: E. T. Meredith III

Cover Photograph: Jim Krantz, Kristsada/Krantz Studio,

All of us at Better Homes and Gardens® Books are dedicated to providing you with information and ideas to enhance your home. We welcome your comments and suggestions. Write to us at:
Better Homes and Gardens Books
Home Decorating and Design
Editorial Department
1716 Locust St.
Des Moines, IA 50309-3023

If you would like to purchase any of our home decorating and design, cooking, crafts, gardening, or home improvement books, check wherever quality books are sold. Or visit us at: bhgbooks.com

contents

1

exploring your options

FEELING A BIT SQUEEZED? Do you dream of a home office, a theater, a gym, a playroom for the kids, or a hobby studio? Look no further than your basement, attic, or the unfinished "bonus" space over your garage. In fact, one of these undervalued parts of your home may be the ideal location for your dream space. Browse these pages to jump-start your ideas. What you'll see are some attractive rooms and suites that grew from humble origins. How much money you spend to transform your basement or attic is up to you. Determine your budget and plan accordingly. In most situations even the grandest projects cost only a fraction of what you'd spend to build an addition.

Use your ingenuity to create a basement living space that's vibrant and comfortable—never plain. A boxy basement requires added architectural interest and dimension. In the basement *opposite*, sheets of plywood have been tinted with raspberry and apricot gel stains, then wall-mounted behind cushioned chairs in the same hues.

Take your style down

You have a sense of style . . . why leave it at ground level? Don't let moisture or light issues get in your way (you'll find solutions to them in later chapters). Low ceilings? Give them a lift with one of many design techniques shown here. If you've always wanted to indulge in a different look, go for it in the basement! Down-under spaces aren't seen from other levels, so there's no need for consistency.

Wine lines

A huge antique champagne poster announces an interest in fine wines. It's not surprising that the contemporary design for this basement entertaining room takes its design cues from a project completed earlier—the wine cellar, *above right*. Slate tiles installed diagonally mimic the lines of the steel zigzagged wine racks. Likewise the track for halogen lights zigzags across the ceiling. Understated bar and back cabinets look like textured black-stained oak but are actually laminate.

Define and distract

Visitors to this arty family room have so many intriguing details to take in, they'll hardly notice that they're in a basement. Exposed joists, covered in teak paneling that once finished the basement walls, add interest to the coffered ceiling, which defines the sitting area and contributes a textural focal point. Lighted display niches draw attention to a collection of pottery.

Take boring out of the box

In their original state most basements have all the allure of a shoebox interior. Rather than settling for boxy or plain, you can enliven these areas with architectural interest and dimension.

■ Mix up the placement of your surfaces. Break out of the boxy mold by varying the height and angle of wall and ceiling planes.

■ Pay attention to lighting. Provide general lighting with track or recessed fixtures. Draw the eye to surfaces; tuck soft uplighting above media cabinets and floating ceilings.

■ Mix materials, textures, and finishes. A coordinated medley of woods, metals, fabrics, and wall finishes imparts excitement. In the basement *above* black steel, maple, and teak mix with a pale green glass and green marble mantel.

Snuggle in

A decorative oval window hovers above the bed, creating a pretty focal point. Soft shapes—such as the window, the round ottoman, and piles of pillows and bedding—relax a room that's made up of angles. Chests of drawers and display space built into the knee walls free up floor space.

Luxury lives at the top

Layers and layers of fabric, imaginative furnishings, and rich color give this master suite a strong—and decidedly French—personality. Napoleon's well-known symbol, the bee, takes on a golden sheen in this bee-emblazoned paper, which initiates the theme of florals and patterns that cozy the room (an adults-only space for parents of four children).

CHECK YOUR ATTIC'S HEADROOM. Most building codes require that a living space be at least 7½ feet high over at least 50 percent of the floor area. When you measure, include the thickness of your finishing materials. If you need more headroom, consider adding a dormer or two.

COMPLEMENT YOUR HOME'S architectural style, especially the exterior. The dormer's classic six-over-six windows *upper right* match those throughout the house.

MAKE THE MOST OF ODD SITUATIONS. You don't need headroom when you're in the bath *lower right*. By placing the tub under the eaves, you free up prime space along the wall for sinks and storage.

THINK MULTIPURPOSE. Ottomans multitask as tables, seating, and footrests. A low bookshelf makes a comfortable window seat.

Sitting pretty

A pair of 10-foot shed dormers opens up an otherwise boxy bedroom. The first dormer *above* creates ample headroom for a spacious sitting area; the second houses a stairwell and the vanity end of the master bath. The built-in bookshelf beneath the bank of windows performs double duty as a window seat.

Surround-free shower

Consider going for the unrestricted feel of an open-design shower *right*. Notice the showerhead and exposed pipes at the ceiling, and the tile surround and drain beneath it. The result is a clean, spacious look, free of curtains and an enclosed surround.

Put a woodsy look in the attic

The dark, faux wood paneling of years past has a bad reputation, but real wood is a wonderful classic. Shown here in a variety of forms from unfinished board-and-batten to stained, pickled, and unfinished planks that run both horizontally and vertically, this old standby adds character to attic spaces. Use paneling to visually tie your attic to paneling used elsewhere in your house or to indulge a new look. Because attics interiors can't be seen from anywhere else in the house, they needn't complement its woodwork.

Board-and-batten

The paneling—broad boards with batten strip covers—and the shape of this attic bedroom recall the 1800s New England character of the home and nearby barn. Dual skylights opposite a bank of windows flood the room with light all day long.

A pitch for pine

Pine reigns in this artist's attic studio/office. The ceiling's 3-inch-wide knotty-pine V-groove paneling has been stained pale blue; the 6-inch wall panels have been pickled white. Ten-inch, unstained pine planks cover the floor. The progression of narrowing plank widths draws the eye upward, making the room seem larger and taller. Crossbeams at the roof peak aren't needed for support; they hold uplights that provide diffused supplemental lighting. During the day four skylights let in plenty of natural light and air.

Wake-up call

A formerly closed-in sleeping porch becomes a breezy guest bedroom with a vaulted ceiling, solid walls, and a prefinished maple floor. The old windows were reglazed rather than replaced to stay within budget. Honey-colored wood blinds darken the room when closed, yet they remain warm- and light-looking.

A bungalow gets a loft

By nabbing unused attic space, a tiny bungalow gains a guest room/studio loft that overlooks a living room's vaulted ceiling. No alterations to the exterior of the home were necessary. Builders first punched through the living room's 8-foot ceiling to the front attic, then tore down attic walls that blocked the flow of light from the sleeping porch. The attic loft upgrades a two-bedroom, 1½-bath bungalow to a wide open three-bedroom, 1¾-bath house, increasing the value of the property.

BUNGALOWS ARE EASY TO OPEN. Their narrow widths and shorter joist spans often require less modification than wider homes, which require more support.

VERIFY EXISTING SUPPORTS. Check with an architect or structural engineer to ensure that the attic floor is strong enough to support a living area and, if not, get suggestions on how to reinforce the floor. Likewise verify the strength of structural roof supports.

INSTALL ROOF VENTS to prevent condensation on the interior of the roof.

A shower with a view

Using the tiny 6x8½-foot bath *below left* is much more refreshing now that it's free of walls and open to blue skies. Given the midloft position of the shower, privacy isn't sacrificed. The glass shower walls offer a view of the tumbled slate tiles. A pine cabinet tucked under the eaves stores towels and toiletries.

No-walls privacy

Just beyond the bath the skylit painter's studio *below* overlooks the living room. The bath's countertop is concrete, poured on-site into a prebuilt frame. It's less expensive than limestone but still offers the natural style of stone. Travertine floor tiles define the bathroom, visually separating the space from the adjoining hall and studio.

Media rooms

A media room takes advantage of a basement's natural assets: darkness, separation from household activity, and shape. Most basements are rectangular, the shape audio-video experts recommend for rich, realistic sound. Those experts also suggest placing rugs or carpet over hard floors. Hard surfaces increase sound distortion; fabrics reduce it.

The long library

A basement-long stretch of bookshelves and cabinets with roll-out drawers organizes books, videos, and compact disks and creates a library-like mood *above*. A comfy sofa and a computer desk provide plenty of space for reading, lounging, or working on projects. Recessed can lighting installed in the ceiling doesn't interfere with the opening and closing of upper cabinetry.

An open-and-shut case

In the center of the library wall *above right* doors open to reveal a television, VCR, and sound system. The opened doors recess into the storage unit while the equipment is in use.

Big-screen country

This basement media room is finished with knotty white pine siding for a comfortable lodge look. Distressed leather furnishings and hollowed-out pine logs that conceal structural steel posts underscore the ambience. Speakers hide under the TV screen, tucked behind black grill cloth and a crating lumber frame. Commercial-grade carpeting and a rubber pad cover the concrete slab. Unlike foam, rubber does not deteriorate in humid conditions.

Media-wise moves

RELATE SCREEN SIZE TO SEATING DISTANCE. For optimum viewing, professional home theater installers recommend a seating distance that's 2 to 2½ times the width of a screen. For example, place sofa and chairs 54 to 68 inches from a 27-inch screen.

FRONT-PROJECTION SYSTEMS replicate the feel of a movie theater but require complete darkness. Rear-projection systems and picture-tube TVs produce a picture that looks good with lights on or off—critical if you're going to party while you watch.

CREATE FULL SURROUND-SOUND WITH FIVE SPEAKERS. Place one speaker on each side of the TV screen, level with your ears when seated, and about 3 feet away from sidewalls.

Place two speakers behind the sofa about 6 to 8 feet off the floor and at least as wide apart as the front pair. Put the fifth one on top of the TV to distribute the dialogue. Action-movie buffs enjoy a subwoofer that intensifies the bass as well as those dramatic booms and bangs. Put it beneath the screen.

STASH EQUIPMENT IN A VENTILATED CABINET so components don't overheat; don't block the vents on the equipment.

CHOOSE DIMMER LIGHT SWITCHES over the toggle style for optimum light control.

FOR HELP FROM A PRO well-versed in the latest technologies and gadgetry, consult a local home theater specialist. Look in the Yellow Pages under "Home Theater" or "Audio/Video."

Fitness rooms

Wedging a fitness routine into your schedule is easy when you have a gym set up at home. Sneak in a yoga session before the kids wake up or do a round of weights while dinner simmers. Your "gym" doesn't need to rival the health club; just make it functional, comfortable, and inviting.

Let's dance

A large attic space is fitted with a wall mirror and barre *above*, creating a studio ideal for doing aerobics or practicing ballet, ballroom dance, or yoga. The space can suit a family of dancers, or a home-based teaching situation. A daybed at the end of the hall is handy for a rest break or for turning the space into guest quarters when needed for overnight visitors.

Go for it!

CHOOSE TOUGH FLOORING such as vinyl, cork or—if carpet is appropriate, a tightly woven style—that cushions your step without impeding your routine.

ENLARGE THE SPACE with a floor-to-ceiling mirror, which also helps you pay attention to your form and technique.

INSTALL ENOUGH OUTLETS. You'll want music and a television/VCR for entertainment and instruction.

POSITION A TELEVISION/VCR for comfortable eye-level viewing while you exercise. For a yoga session place the TV just off the floor.

DON'T FORGET VENTILATION. Install a fan and several operable windows.

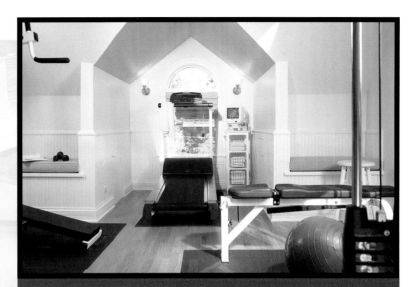

Go lift upstairs

The intriguing architecture of attics—peaked ceilings and angled dormers and walls—makes them inspiring places to lift weights. Fitted with ceiling fans, properly placed windows for ventilation, and a backup air-conditioner or fan, attics become comfortable places for workouts too.

Get buff in the basement

Durable vinyl flooring and an energizing color scheme create an attractive space for many exercise routines. A small bump-out topped with a greenhouse window draws in lots of light. Check out the exterior view of this space on page 30.

Just my size

Kids love snug spaces, which makes this attic nook a desirable child's retreat. A low window bench and cushy pillows tempt kids to curl up with a book—or stage a squadron of action figures. When it's time to clean up, toys stash away easily in the under-eaves closets.

Playrooms

Children are thrilled by any space in which they can indulge their imaginations. That includes wide-open spaces good for spreading out and setting up art tables, racetracks, and theaters, or a secret nook where they can burrow in and dream. Whatever type of space your project involves, think ahead to when the little kids will be bigger. If you're finishing unfinished space now, spare yourself greater expense by installing any wiring, plumbing, or soundproofing you may want later.

More clever than costly

Candy-colored wall paint and black-and-white sheet vinyl flooring easily invigorate this block wall/cement slab play space *below*. Another standout feature is the ceiling treatment: Wave after wave of polka-dot fabric stapled to floor joists creates a party-tent effect and conceals pipes.

Hardy color

Primary-colored vinyl tiles, rugs, hardware, and trim paint punctuate the durable white vinyl floors and cabinetry of this spacious basement walkout play area *above*. Although it's currently equipped with kid-scaled furnishings, the area can easily become an art studio, exercise room, or party place as the family's needs change.

Kid smarts

MAKE THE SPACE SAFE. Fit attic windows with childproof locks; fit basement spaces with an egress window or exit. CHOOSE DURABLE, easy-to-clean wall and floor treatments. MOUNT A BIG MIRROR securely on the wall; children love to play in front of them. (Keep it away from the scooters, though.)

ENCOURAGE CLEANUP with see-through storage solutions. Shelves, stacking bins, and hooks make it easy for kids to find their favorite things and remember what goes where. STIMULATE PLAY with high-contrast color schemes. Black-and-white and vibrant, opposing colors are energizing.

Home offices and work spaces

Every home needs an office. If you doubt it, ask someone who has tried to manage the family finances, correspondence, travel plans, and daily logistics from the kitchen counter. Not only adults but kids too need a place to study and work. Fully functioning offices can be tucked in the thinnest slivers of space, but look to your basement or attic if you need room to spread out.

Mark your space

Who needs walls? Tucked under a staircase, a knotty pine headband, a funky, painted pillar, and black-and-white tiles define the work space in this teen suite, *right*. In just a few square feet there's room for an L-shape desk, shelving, and a computer and its peripherals.

Designed to graduate

A chalkboard wall (it's actually chalkboard paint), a run of built-in desks, and school-style pendant lights create a charming learning center *below*. As the family's needs change, shelves can be cleared to make way for books or home office materials.

Mix it up

Treetop attics have what it takes to create quiet, light-filled offices. The office *above* was furnished with a ready-to-assemble (RTA) desk and storage components. RTA furniture is a boon if access to the attic is tight because you can carry up the pieces and assemble them in place. Mixing materials—black metal, wicker basket drawers, and stylish fabric covers—creates a textural, eclectic look that's full of visual surprise. The office chair hardly looks run-of-the-mill with a kick-pleated chair dress.

The long-wall advantage

No pipes, ductwork, or stairs were moved to create the home office *right*. Built around an exterior wall devoted to storage, the shelving/desk unit provides room for two to work or meet with clients. No one recognizes the standard basement windows. Note the one *far right*, worked into the storage wall and set off with eggplant-color paint. A glass entry door at one end of the office provides a safe exit to the outdoors.

Studios and workshops

Away from the core of household activity, basements and attics make wonderful locations for exploring creative interests. You'll marvel at the inspiration that comes from having a place dedicated to your craft, a place where all your tools and materials are close at hand and easy to use. So claim your space and get creative.

Inspiration down under

Fitted with French doors and a tiled floor, the walkout basement *above* is an elegant, light-filled painter's studio. Throw open the windows and pull up a table, and the space quickly converts to an alfresco dining area.

The dream shop

By placing an exhaust fan in the window and hooking equipment to dust-collection systems, the home shop *top right* stays extra clean. The wall-hung cabinets are mounted over the pegboard wall on support strips, so the cabinets can be lifted and moved to new locations as shop needs change.

A place for everything

A family of crafters revels in their bonus room turned workshop. They can see what's available to work with at a glance, thanks to a wall of white modular shelving units and masses of see-though boxes, bins, and letter trays that organize colorful supplies and tools. The big laminate table, an easy-to-clean surface, provides enough room for everyone to gather around.

Boost your creativity

PREVENT MUSCLE FATIGUE that comes from standing on hard surfaces by placing soft, nonslip rubber mats where you'll be working (available at restaurant supply outlets). If you don't like the look, toss decorative rugs over them.

DEDICATE ELECTRICAL CIRCUITS to individual pieces of equipment and route them through a subpanel with a master switch that allows you to turn off the power to all equipment when the shop is not in use.

SOUNDPROOF YOUR WORKSHOP if your work is noisy (or if your work requires peace and quiet). Install a fan and at least two operable windows for ventilation and to remove fumes.

Bonus rooms

Garage-top bonus spaces—the result of keeping garage rooflines in scale with the main residence—are increasingly common with newer homes. Attached to the house, these areas hold vast potential as private studies, studios, and even spas. As part of a separate structure, they recall carriage houses of old, perfect for expansive offices and in-law or guest suites.

Imaginative kids benefit from a clubhouse *below* and *right* that fills the bonus space over the garage. The design, however, is smart: Although kid gear fills the place now, the cabinetry, fixtures, lighting, and built-in storage can serve many different functions. Later on the clubhouse can be transformed into a teen hangout, guest suite, creative studio, or adult retreat.

Roughhouse style

School lockers, beanbag chairs, and particleboard floor tiles set the scene for activity in this playroom-clubhouse (and they're budget-savvy to boot). Modular storage components harbor oodles of toys, games, and videos, and also house the television. Oversize stuffed animals keep an eye on activities from their shelf-top perch.

A place of your own

A kitchenette makes for great pizza parties and sleep-over bagel breakfasts. The sleeping loft *above* has a ladder that can be pulled up for privacy or to zone off the space from inquisitive toddlers. A ledge at the loft and a huge kitchen tackboard yield plenty of display space for favorite objects and artwork.

Follow the vines up the stairs to the garage-top clubhouse *left*. It boasts a kitchenette, loft, and full bath—all in just 40 square feet.

assessing your available space

RIGHT NOW YOU'RE PROBABLY SITTING OVER—or under—some potential living space: your basement, attic, or the bonus room over your garage. Don't let the presence of moisture, or a lack of light or headroom, deter you from taking advantage of these spaces. Sure, they probably look like giant storerooms right now, and doubtless they have some challenges that need to be resolved. Read on to learn what deterrents can be put to rest. You'll discover an invaluable partner in your local building official, who can tell you what building codes apply to your project. In doing so you'll understand the potential of your space and produce a successful transformation.

Floor space is limited in the attic master bedroom *opposite,* but the unusually steep roofline and peak make for plenty of headroom. Banks of windows capture views and welcome light to give the room an expansive feel despite its small size. Wall-mounted reading lamps at either side of the bed free tabletops for books. An upholstered chair sits between the bed and closet, creating a comfortable place to put on shoes.

Dry ideals

The task of drying out a basement can be as straightforward as clearing clogged gutters and downspouts, and keeping them in proper alignment. It can cost as little as some elbow grease and a can of waterproofing medium. More elaborate measures, such as installing a sump pump or exterior water-proofing, cost a few hundred to a few thousand dollars—nominal sums when you compare the cost of moving or adding on. Even if your basement is dry, it pays to make sure a drainage system is in place and up-to-date. For step-by-step instructions on how to solve the issue of a wet basement, turn to page 140.

Dream ahead and save

Maybe you know exactly what you want for your basement, attic, or bonus room project. But before you commit to building that playroom, bedroom, home office, workshop, or media room, invest some time thinking about your family's future needs and desires. The space you tap for a playroom now may be best used as a home office or a full guest suite with bath and minikitchen later. Save substantial amounts of money and simplify the transition by having the necessary wiring, plumbing, and mechanical work either finished or roughed in before you cover the walls. Even if you don't plan to live in your home forever, your planning goes a long way toward boosting the value of your house.

Before you start building, run through the room function checklist below to discover any unmet needs to include in your plans. Then imagine your family 5, 10, 15, even 20 years from now and do a mental run-through of the checklist for each time period. Use this information as you plot features, supply lines, and outlets.

- Master suite
- Full living suite for an extended family member or caretaker
- Family or guest bedrooms (with or without attached bath)
- Living/gathering space
- Bar or party area
- Home office
- Family computing and homework area
- Children's play space
- Workshop or studio for creative pursuits
- Wine cellar
- Library
- Media room
- Exercise center
- Laundry, storage areas

Yes, it's a basement

Deep, operable windows open into a well whose walls are finished with the same siding that covers the house. Even though these windows are below grade-level, they fill the room with light. If you like you can place plants or garden art in the well outside the window to create a view.

Step out safely
Building code requires windows with wells deeper than 44 inches to be fitted with steps *left* or a ladder. Transform the steps into a garden until they're needed for escape.

Greenhouse effect
Much like a dormer draws light into an attic, greenhouse windows installed over a basement bumpout *below* fill a below-grade space with light. See interior on page 17.

Light up the dark

In the basement the solution to gloom can be as simple as putting in a big window or two. Natural light makes your basement space seem more expansive and cheerful. Place basement windows facing east to capture morning light, and south for all-day exposure. West-facing windows will obviously pull in warmer afternoon sun—something to avoid in warmer climates. If a new opening needs to be cut in the foundation to accept a larger window, it's probably best to get a pro's help with installation.

Paired with a well, below-grade windows draw in nearly as much light as their above-grade counterparts. What about the view? Your window well, which may be as few as 12 inches deep and finished with a ready-made steel insert or as deep as you like (width is infinite, for example, at a basement walkout), is the answer. Finish it with masonry or a step garden planted with low-maintenance plants or garden ornaments, or greenhouse windows. If you can see your basement windows from the yard or street, match the type and style of your above-grade windows for consistency.

You can balance natural basement window light with a faux lighted window. A faux window creates the illusion of sunlight; make one by mounting lightbulbs in a window cutout that's covered with frosted plexiglass, trimmed, then dressed with shutters, blinds, or sheer drapery panels. See page 53 for detailed instructions.

In an attic the solutions to dark spaces are the same, but with a variation. Place windows on gable-end walls and in dormers to light the space. You also can use skylights to draw in light, fresh air, and spectacular upward-angled views that aren't possible anywhere else in the house.

In addition to natural light, basement and attic rooms need liberal doses of general and task lighting for use in the evening. Ask the staff at your local lighting store or home center to help you plot a blend of recessed cans, track lighting, hanging fixtures, and lamps according to how you'll use the room.

Let the sun pour in

An operable skylight is placed strategically over an attic stairwell *above* for views of mature trees outside. The window draws air through the house and pulls in lots of light.

Patio within a window well

Fill your below-grade rooms with light by installing French-style sliding glass doors that open onto a window-well patio *left*. Three- and 4-foot wells don't claim much space but are big enough for a collection of plants or a small grill.

Look past a low ceiling

The International Residential Code requires basement and attic rooms to have a minimum ceiling height of 7 feet (84 inches) over at least 50 percent of the floor area. Bathrooms, hallways, and task areas can have ceilings that dip as low as 76 inches in some spots (see "Building code savvy" on page 36 for information). Find out whether the area that you're considering remodeling has enough room to create a new living area by measuring the distance between the floor and the bottom of the ceiling joists. Subtract a cou-ple of inches from your figures to allow for finished floor and ceiling materials.

After you satisfy ceiling-height requirements, use fool-the-eye tricks to make low ceilings seem taller. A strong focal point such as a fireplace, a media center, or an oversize work of art—even a pretty window view—attracts attention and distracts the eye from low ceilings. When possible, place the focal point low to the floor or at seated eye level where it's most effective. Windows and glass doors that offer "through-views" beyond the room's perimeter visually open a space.

Need headroom?

If your attic is short on the headroom-over-floor space requirement, you can often meet it by adding one or more dormers. A shed dormer is shown *left*. Fitted with windows, dormers draw in loads of light and enhance your home's architectural interest inside and out.

Rest on the low side

Placing the bed length along the knee wall *below* frees high-ceiling space for dressing and other activities in this smaller attic bedroom. Window light and a night table and lamp serve the cushy chair too.

Enough room for high style
Claiming an attic gable end makes plenty of room for the luxurious bath *above left*. A mirrored wall makes the room feel even larger.

Tall walls from the start
The owners of the walkout basement *above right* always planned to finish it, so they arranged for a tall ceiling from the start. Note the mirror on tracks over the fireplace. It moves up the track when the firebox is in use, and drops down as an attractive cover when it's not.

A bath *will* fit in the basement or attic

If you have just a sliver of headroom, you can include a bathroom in your basement or attic project. Headroom is generally required only over half the floor space in a room, and fortunately, you don't need full headroom over a toilet or the head end of a tub. The simplest and least costly way to create a basement or attic bath is to locate it directly above, below, or back-to-back with the main plumbing stack. If that's not possible you'll need to connect your toilet and bath drain to the main stack with a branch drain. Attic joists usually have plenty of space between them to run the drain from the bath to the stack; in the basement you can either cut out and excavate beneath part of the basement floor to install a branch drain, or if you have sufficient headroom, elevate the bathroom floor and run plumbing beneath it.

Build a better basement
If you're building a new house, boost your home's value from the get-go by having your builder dig a foundation for a 9- or 10-foot ceiling instead of the standard 7 or 8. The extra cost is nominal. Even if you don't finish the basement, your home's future owners will appreciate the headroom and the potential that it yields. If you like that idea, bypass the standard basement windows from the start, too, and install full-egress windows.

Park the guests
An unused garage nestled in a garden setting *below* creates an innovative space in which to gather guests. The floors are finished with tile, but the wall and ceiling frames are left exposed for a woody, utilitarian look that works in a mild climate.

JOSEFFA
USEPPA ISLAND

Straighten curves, cracks

Slight curves or cracks in basement walls and attic rafters and floors don't have to put a stop to your remodeling plans. Study those cracks and curves more closely and you'll see that you can probably correct them.

BASEMENT WALLS After a house is built, soil moves and settles around its foundation, putting pressure on even the sturdiest of basement walls. Minor cracks don't indicate a weak foundation, but they sometimes admit moisture and radon. (See page 140 for information on rectifying moisture

problems, and page 99 for radon detection and solutions.)

It's possible to straighten bowed basement walls, but doing so may call for steel bracing. Consult a licensed building or remodeling contractor who specializes in basement repair before attempting the job. Search directories for "Foundation Contractors."

ATTIC RAFTERS Sagging rafters indicate one of two problems: too many layers of roofing or insufficiently sized rafters. To check for sag stretch a string from the bottom edge at the top of the rafter to the bottom edge at the bottom of the rafter; then measure the sag at the midpoint. The occasional sagging rafter (with midpoint drop of ¼ to ½ inch) may do so because of a crack or open knothole. Straighten the rafter by bolting a 2×4 over the damage. With more sag, a rafter must be jacked back into place, a job for a professional. If, on the other hand, you find a run of rafters that are sagging, you may need to install a structural knee wall to support them (see page 162).

ATTIC FLOORS Check exposed floor-joist sag in the attic using the same technique you used to check for rafter sag. If you suspect sagging, structural support for the area may have been removed over the years, i.e., if previous homeowners removed or rearranged load-bearing walls. Consult a building contractor or engineer to plan the appropriate beams, posts, or walls to support the floor.

Finish a bonus room like an attic

Bonus rooms are generally unfinished spaces that top a garage, the result of keeping garage rooflines in scale with the main residence. Bonus rooms and attics share characteristics, the primary one being open space beneath a pitched roof. When you're remodeling a bonus room, use the same assessment and technique guidelines as you used for an attic.

Think twice about converting your garage

When pressed for living space, you may be tempted to convert your garage. Garage floors are easily finished, walls are already framed, and there's ready access to the outdoors. But the list of disadvantages is just as long. You'll need to find another place to park the cars and store everything that was previously stashed in the garage. Reworking the garage exterior so it looks like the rest of the house is a costly job, as is ripping up and redirecting the drive so it doesn't direct visitors into your new living space. If you don't replace the garage or make these revisions, the value of your property may take a nose dive. Proceed with caution! A local real estate agent or appraiser can advise you.

Check for sag

Use a tape measure, thumbtacks, and a taut string as described in text and shown *below* to check for sag in rafters and floor joists. The odd rafter with a bit of sag can be jacked into place; if there are several you may need to put in a structural knee wall for support. Sagging ceiling joists can require an engineer and architect's expertise.

building code savvy

Put codes to work for you

Building codes are designed to protect the structural integrity of your home, safeguarding your health and safety and that of your family, friends, and anyone who comes in contact with your home. Before you plan a remodeling project, visit your city's building department. Doing so helps move your ideas forward and may well be one of the most enlightening 15 minutes that you invest in your project. Be prepared to tell the officials what you'd like to do—even if your ideas are rough—and ask them what building codes apply. A rough sketch of the available space, as well as the location of windows, doors, and mechanical systems, makes your visit even more productive. Don't be discouraged if local codes call for a standard you can't meet. If safety or practicality isn't compromised, many officials are willing to make exceptions to accommodate existing buildings.

WHO'S YOUR BUILDING OFFICIAL? Your governing building official and codes likely are located in the building department of your town or city government. If you live outside city limits, this function may be performed at the county level by the clerk or commissioner. In some circumstances county officials do not govern a property, and you'll need to call the state departments of building standards or housing to find a governing official.

PERMITS AND INSPECTIONS If you're changing the function of a space—converting a storage-focused basement, attic, or bonus room into living space, for example—you need a building permit. You'll also need one if you're changing your home's shape or entries, moving mechanical functions, or changing how your home relates to utility supply lines. To obtain a building permit, include a legal description of your property; a drawing that indicates changes, materials, and dimensions; and a site plan drawing that shows your house in relation to neighboring houses, wells, and septic systems. This information can be obtained from your property deed or city or county records. You can do the drawings yourself.

Small projects may only require a final inspection, but more complex projects usually require several inspections. You or your contractor will be responsible for calling to arrange inspections before the work to be evaluated becomes

A tip and a caution

Take a tip from experienced remodelers: By involving your local building official in your project plans from the start, you gain a welcome, helpful partner who will likely help you work with the building code to get what you want from your project and obtain a building permit. Don't put yourself at significant financial risk and safety by remodeling without a building permit. If your project is eventually revealed, inspected, and not up to code, you may be asked to rework it, accruing untold expense. A remodel that's not up to code may be revealed when you go to sell your house, negatively affecting your home being sold.

covered by further work. For example, have your foundation trench and forms checked before pouring concrete; have your drywall nailing pattern checked before taping and mudding. Roofing is checked upon completion.

SPECIFIC BUILDING CODES Need a starting point for a discussion with your building official? According to the International Residential Code produced by the International Code Council, the elements noted in the box below are commonly governed by most building codes. Codes applying to your home may be different. Codes specify minimum standards; for safety or comfort; you may want to exceed what the codes require.

Common inspections

INSPECTION	WHAT'S REVIEWED
Foundation alterations	Trench, forms
Beneath the floor	Floor, framing, utility lines
Framing	Lumber grade, connectors such as joist hangers
Rough plumbing	Pipe sizes, materials
Rough wiring	Wire sizes, boxes, workmanship
Roofing	Materials, flashing
Energy efficiency	Insulation, window area
Interior walls	Wallboard nailing pattern
Flues/fireplace	Clearances, materials
Gas line	Fittings, pressure test
Finished project	Electrical and plumbing fixtures, railings, furnace, smoke detectors

Befriend your building official

Your building official may become a key partner in getting the basement space you dream of. Pay a visit early to find out what codes might apply to your basement project. Codes have relaxed recently, so if your project requires a variance from code, your building official may be able to help you get it—if safety is not compromised.

Office in a wedge

This L-shape office area sits opposite a TV/conversation space. Although both spaces wedge beneath low-ceiling portions of the attic area, the situation meets code because the spaces open to each other. The high-ceiling area that covers 50 percent of the room is found above the passageway in between the two spaces.

Building codes gain consistency

Building codes may be getting more consistent. Cities, towns, and municipalities are free to choose the building codes they adhere to; what's permissible in one location isn't necessarily permissible in another. But in recent years three of the country's largest building code organizations* have combined forces to create the International Code Council (ICC) and a coordinated, comprehensive set of building codes called the I-Codes to serve the nation. The I-Codes were completed in 2000, and many municipalities across the country have quickly adopted them. If you're remodeling a basement, attic, or bonus room, three of

the ICC codes may apply to your project: the building, residential, and zoning codes. In general the I-Codes are less restrictive with some issues, such as ceiling height (if a standard door opens into the space, the ceiling height is OK) and more conservative with respect to safety issues. For more information contact your local building department or the International Code Council at www.intlcode.org or at 703/931-4533.

*The International Conference of Building Officials (ICBO), the Building Officials and Code Administrators (BOCA), and the Southern Building Code Council International, Inc. (SBCCI).

Code know-how

ROOM HEIGHT: Habitable spaces—those rooms used for living, sleeping, eating, and cooking—must be no less than 7 feet high. There are at least three exceptions to this particular rule:

- TO ACCOMMODATE SLOPING CEILINGS in an attic, the 7-foot ceiling height requirement must be met over 50 percent of the floor area. Ceiling height must be no less than 5 feet at any point in the room. (This may mean putting knee walls in attic conversions where the roofline runs down to the floor.)

- BEAMS, GIRDERS, AND PROJECTIONS that are spaced no less than 4 feet on center may drop no more than 6 inches below the ceiling height.

- CEILINGS IN BASEMENTS used for nonhabitable purposes can be 6 feet, 8 inches, with beams, girders, and other projections yielding a ceiling clearance of no less than 6 feet, 4 inches.

ROOM FLOOR SPACE: The I-Codes maintain that habitable rooms for living, sleeping, eating, and cooking must measure at least 7×7 feet. That's a pretty tiny room. Take a look at the box *below right* on room size recommendations for a better idea of appropriate measurements.

LIGHT, VENTILATION, AND SAFE EXIT: Habitable rooms must have window square footage that measures 8 percent of the room's total square footage. For ventilation, half the window square footage amount must be operable. As an example, a 100-square-foot room measuring 10×10 feet requires 8 square feet of windows with 4 square feet of operable area. If the ventilation requirement can't be met with windows, then doors, louvers, vents, and even mechanical devices, such as a furnace vent, can be used, but your building official will need to agree on sufficient provisions.

For safe exits in the event of fire, all sleeping rooms above or below grade are required to have either a door to the outside or a window with 5.7 square feet of operable area through which a person can escape. Window wells that are 44 inches below grade level must have a permanent ladder or steps. Building code standards aside, it makes good sense to provide plenty of safe exits whether a room is intended for sleeping or not. Exterior stairs from attic escape windows *are not* required, but you'd be wise to store a flexible emergency ladder nearby nonetheless.

SMOKE, FIRE, AND GAS SAFETY: Building code requires the installation of a smoke detector in every sleeping room and in hallways that lead to them. Ironically carbon monoxide detectors are not required by code, but you may want to install one near sleeping areas on every level of your home. Better yet place one next to the smoke detector in every bedroom. Building codes also govern construction materials for fire safety.

OTHER ELEMENTS are also governed by codes, so discuss your plans fully with your building official. Kitchens and baths and the features that go with them, for instance, have their own set of codes—so discuss those too. Here are a few general features that you'll probably want to discuss with your building official:

STAIRS: Tread, riser, headroom measurements, plus handrail shape and location.

GENERAL CONSTRUCTION: Lumber specifications, stud and joist spacing, nail and screw types and spacing.

MECHANICALS: Electric cable type, number and placement of receptacles; ground-fault circuit interrupters (GFCIs); plumbing pipe material (copper, plastic, steel) and size, solder type, venting, traps, and connections.

Room size recommendations

The U.S. Department of Housing and Urban Development recommends the following sizes for particular rooms. Minimum net floor area is within enclosed walls (excluding built-in features, such as cabinets and closets).

	MIN AREA	MIN SIZE	PREFERRED
Master bedroom	n/a	n/a	12×16
Bedroom	80 sq. ft.	8×10	11×14
Family room	110 sq. ft.	10.5×10.5	12×16
Living room	176 sq. ft.	11×16	12×18
Great room	n/a	n/a	14×20
Bathroom	35 sq. ft.	5×7	5×9

Turning your idea into reality

The task of remodeling your basement, attic, or bonus room might feel overwhelming, but the undertaking is much less so when it's broken down into bite-size steps. Take a look at the progression of work that follows; then keep this list handy, both as a reassuring guide and as a measure of the progress you're making as your project moves along.

COLLECT IDEAS. Get a sense of what others have done with their basements, attics, and bonus rooms. You already started this phase by perusing Chapter 1 of this book, but don't stop there. Flip through magazines, books, and brochures for more. Get a three-ring binder, and outfit it with a bunch of three-ring pocket folders. When you see an idea you like, clip it and drop it into a binder folder. Mark clippings so you remember what you liked about them—maybe a layout, surface material, or decorative technique. As thoughts come to you, jot down notes about why you want to finish your space and your ideas for using it. Assign a pocket to those notes as well. You'll feel more confident knowing that you don't have to remember these ideas because you've safely stored them in your binder. Devote at least a month to this phase—some people spend a year or two in this stage. If you do spend that much time, you get a good sense of what you like, and you'll move on to the next stage when your needs for additional living space begin to demand more attention.

GATHER FACTS about your available space and your needs. Local real estate appraisers can help you get a feel for improvements that are wise given your neighborhood. The time to get a real feel for your basement, attic, or bonus room's transformation potential is *before* your need for space reaches critical mass. "Building code savvy" on page 36 can help. That's where you learn about visiting your city's building department to discuss your space and needs in broad-brush terms, and find out what's possible and what's not. You'll also determine whether your space is weathertight and, if not, how to take the steps to make it so. See "Diagnosing moisture problems" on page 140 for more

details. Many homeowners weatherproof their unfinished spaces—basements in particular—and test them through a few seasons to be confident they're ready for transformation when the time comes. And there's no time like the present to work through the section "Bids, estimates, and money" on page 94; it helps draw your needs and wants into clearer focus.

START YOUR IDEA MACHINE. You know your space; you know your needs. Put them together and start shaping possibilities—start sketching some initial floor plans. Get a sense of how you can possibly draw light into the basement, gain headroom in the attic, and fit full-service bathrooms in both. Chapter 3 is your key plan-development resource. This phase of the job is a great time to call on an architect or building designer for help, as their experienced eyes often see solutions you may overlook. Even if you get outside design help, you can still do as much of the actual work as you like. Plan to spend several weeks to several months in the idea-crafting stage. You'll live with the results for many years, so it's a good investment. If you need to jazz up the space in the meantime, check out "Quick fix-ups" on page 54 for ideas on bridging the gap between unfinished and finished spaces.

CHECK OUT MATERIALS. Shopping for materials before your plans are fine-tuned may seem premature, but the fact is that what you choose in terms of both construction and surface materials—has an impact on your final plans. So collect those ideas and drop them into your binder. Chapter 4 *Materials* gets you started. You may have been looking at materials from the moment you decided to remodel, or maybe not. Spend some time thinking about what you plan to use before you move on to the next stage.

MOVE YOUR PLANS TOWARD DETAIL. Rough plans need to become firm in order to become implemented. You need to figure every detail—from storage and utilities to finishing methods and decorative trims. If you go this far on your own designing the space, this is an excellent time to have an architect or building designer review your plans to spare you the headaches of oversights later. Give yourself a couple of months in this phase. Chapter 5 *Fine-Tuning Your Plan* helps you move from the planning stage to the implementation stage. Now you're getting somewhere!

DETERMINE WHO WILL DO THE WORK. Perhaps you want to do the remodeling work yourself, or maybe you've always planned to hire it out. Now is the time to give the topic serious consideration, to track down your general contractor or subcontractors, and to prepare your space for transformation. The section "Who will do the work?"on page 92 walks you through these decisions. If you're doing all or part of the work yourself, consult Chapter 6 *Tools* to see whether you have what you need for the tasks you'll complete. Allow a couple months for this stage.

PREPARE FOR DOING THE WORK. If you're doing the work yourself, it's time to apply for building permits (see "Building code savvy" on page 36) and prepare a calendar of work, material-ordering dates, and inspections that will take place along the way. Building permits are good for only a limited amount of time; discuss this aspect, plus inspections, with your city's building department. It's also time to prepare the rest of your home for the remodeling effort: Relocate activities, re-route entries, protect traffic routes through the house, arrange for dumpsters, if necessary. A couple of weeks is all you need, if that, for this effort.

ORDER MATERIALS. You'll need to order materials several times throughout the project, arranging for them to arrive when you need them but not before. The exception to this is arranging for joists and sheet goods that are difficult to carry into attic spaces. In such instances (these are identified in Chapter 9 *Remodeling Your Attic*), you can arrange to get these goods into the attic during construction of a dormer. (If no dormer is being added, you may need to make a temporary opening in the roof to get the materials to the site. See page 158 for details.)

STRAP ON YOUR TOOL BELT and start your project. Feels good, doesn't it? Your project is now under way! The first order of business is to take care of demolition and do major structural and mechanical work. That means building stairs, moving mechanical elements, re-routing utility lines, roughing in ductwork and underfloor drains, and replacing old plumbing.

FRAME YOUR ROOMS. Now is the time to reinforce joists and install subfloors, exterior doors, dormers, and windows. After you frame the rooms and install interior doors, the skeleton of your finished space is complete. Use Chapters 7, 8, and 9 to plan your work. The length of time this and any of the following steps require varies depending on the scope and complexity of the project, the time you have available to work, and whether you're working alone or with a helper. (If you hire out the work, the process moves more quickly, of course.)

INSTALL INTERNAL SYSTEMS. After the walls are framed in, run the wires, pipes, and ducts for water, gas, electric, and climate control. Install nail plates on framing pieces to prevent nails from being inadvertently driven through utility lines. It's a good idea to take pictures of the lines in place at this point, lest you forget to mark them on the covering drywall. Finally insulate the walls—including interior walls that you want to soundproof. Turn to Chapter 7 *Techniques* for detailed how-to guidance for these installations.

ADD THOSE FINISHING TOUCHES. Your project is in the homestretch! This is when you install wall and ceiling surfaces—typically drywall, but occasionally paneling or a suspended ceiling for a basement. Then it's time to paint and install trim and flooring. Find the how-to information for these surface treatment in Chapter 10 *Finishing Touches*.

CELEBRATE THE FINISH! Your new space is complete! Commemorate your planning and hard work with a gathering and a toast in its honor. Have someone take your photo in the new space. Tuck photographs of the project's progression into a photo album, or use your planning binder as an album. Share your efforts and hard work with friends and family!

3

developing your design ideas

YOU'RE ON YOUR WAY to creating a fabulous new living space in your existing home. By now you've seen what others have done and you've determined that your basement, attic, or bonus room has the potential to become a finished part of your inviting home. Move your dreams toward reality by addressing some functional elements now—the things that make you comfortable and at ease in a space, such as stairs, windows, light, and temperature control. You'll find plenty of things to do to fuel your ideas. Take planning one step at a time, as this chapter demonstrates, and you'll find that it's a pleasure.

Honey-stained hardwood flooring, plenty of light, and a silk ficus tree give this basement bedroom a fresh look; dark furnishings add richness. But the key to this room's success? Fluorescent tubes mounted behind the shuttered wall bathes the room in soft, natural-looking light. The shutters also add textural interest and provide a backdrop from which to hang artwork.

stepping into
your new place

Start thinking about stairs as soon as you decide to create new living space in your basement or attic. Their placement affects the layout of all other room elements. Building codes for stairs that lead to nonhabitable spaces such as unfinished basements and attics are different from those for stairs going to habitable rooms, so you'll probably need to make some changes. If existing stairs don't measure up to code, you can either remake them in the same location or build new stairs

Stair smarts

Don't let that angled space beneath the stairs sit idle. Use it to house the TV and other media equipment. In the basement *above*, folding doors inset with sheer fabric conceal media equipment when it's not in use. Understair space can be configured for lots of other uses as well (see "Plan your storage" on page 88). To create a focal point, you can fit it with a mass of lighted architectural display cubes for showcasing collections. In a supporting storage role, set it up with a combination of broad drawers and pullout hanging rods. Or use the same approach as modern pullout kitchen pantries and turn the space into a library with a series of pullout carts.

Stair-positioning tips

LOCATE STAIRS LEADING TO MULTIPURPOSE attics or basements, so people don't have to walk through a bedroom or bath to reach a public room.
PLACE STAIRS LEADING TO FAMILY ROOMS and recreation rooms near the kitchen.
AVOID CONNECTING NOISY ROOMS TO QUIET ONES. If it can't be avoided, soundproof the stairwell by insulating the walls that surround it.
STAIRS BUILT PARALLEL TO CEILING JOISTS take less time to install and require fewer cuts and fewer materials than those stairs built perpendicular to ceiling joists.

in a different location. Codes vary with stair configurations and railing shape, so ask your building official about them (see "Building code savvy" on page 36).

Stair shapes

If a straight run of stairs doesn't suit you or your space, consider other shapes.

STRAIGHT-RUN STAIRS take up about 40 square feet of floor space at the lower level.

L- OR U-SHAPE STAIRS claim more floor area but are a good choice when a straight run is too steep.

SPIRAL STAIRS are often used for getting to lofts and retreats. They're generally 4 to 6 feet in diameter, so they have the advantage of taking up very little floor space. Because it's difficult to move large objects or furnishings up them, building code often prohibits them from leading to rooms larger than 400 square feet.

WINDER STAIRCASES eliminate the need for a landing around a sharp turn.

straight

l-shape

spiral

winder

u-shape

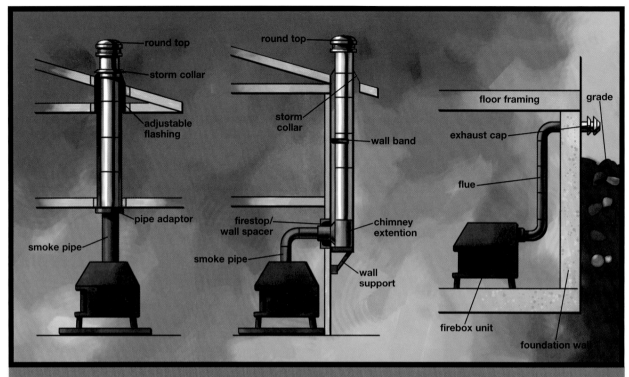

Venting a wood- or gas-burning heater

A wood-burning heater or fireplace vents directly through the roof *left* or along the outside of the house *middle* with a flue pipe that extends above the roofline. A direct-vent, gas-burning heater or fireplace *right* vents directly through the exterior wall, making for an easy, inexpensive installation.

You probably call it a furnace but, in the field, it's a heating, ventilation, and air-conditioning system—an HVAC system, for short. If your converted basement or attic is well insulated, your current system probably can handle the job of serving the new space. Ask the technician who inspects and cleans your unit. If your existing system is sufficient, plan to run ducts or pipes through the walls to the new space, or run them up the walls or across the ceiling and box them in with framing and drywall. (In many cases an existing HVAC system is able to adequately heat a renovated attic—heat rises—but is hard-pressed to cool it sufficiently.)

If your HVAC system isn't up to the added load, you have a couple of choices: Upgrade to a larger-capacity system or install a separate heating and/or cooling source (electric or gas heater, gas fireplace, wood-burning stove, or room air-conditioner). In recent years these appliances have become more efficient, safe, quiet, and attractive than ever before, and they offer very efficient and easy-to-install options.

Ceiling fans also are effective at cooling a room and circulating warm air. Ceiling-hugger and pendant-drop models accommodate various ceiling heights and situations. WINDOWS ALSO AFFECT COOLING and ventilation. Plan windows so they aid ventilation by drawing a breeze from one side of the room to another.

Clearances for mechanical equipment

Place mechanical equipment, such as furnaces, water heaters, and softeners, in a room of their own, or let them share space with the laundry and shop. Most appliances require air space above and around the housing; check the user's manual or contact the manufacturer to obtain this information. Ensure a mechanical room has its own light switch near the entrance. Doors to such spaces must be big enough to move the largest piece of equipment in or out and never less than 20 inches wide. Allow for a clear workspace, 30 inches wide by 30 inches tall, near the furnace control panel.

LANDSCAPE FEATURES have a surprisingly beneficial effect on heating and cooling. Trees planted to the east of your house shade it from morning sun; trees to the west shade it in the afternoon. Consider planting deciduous trees, whose leaves offer shade during hot summers, then drop for the cold season, letting winter's sun bathe the house in warmth. Evergreens planted on the north side of the house offer protection from winter winds.

Insulation

Your HVAC system works much more effectively when your rooms are properly insulated. For more information on insulating basement walls, see page 148; for insulating attics, see page 169. Insulation materials are relatively inexpensive, and the comfort and energy savings they yield make them one of the best investments you can make for your new living space.

Warm up to a fireplace

You can't beat the ambience that a fireplace provides. Put one in, and you won't have any trouble coaxing people down or up the stairs. Direct-vent gas fireplaces are an excellent choice; they're easy to install, can be used as a backup heat source, and produce no messy ash. Regardless of the style you choose, you'll find them available in a variety of looks, sizes, heat output levels, and prices.

DIRECT-VENT GAS FIREPLACES connect to existing gas lines; LP-fired models are also available. These units offer a combination of aesthetics, efficiency, safety, and ease of installation. They're vented to the outdoors using a short length of two-in-one pipe that carries combustion byproducts out and draws in fresh air for combustion. The pipe can make two right-angle turns without losing any efficiency. You can choose a fireplace that's freestanding or ready for framing; it may be more decorative in function or one that's intended to provide heat. One big perk to having a gas fireplace in your home is that it can provide some heat (and some provide quite a lot—check the BTU output ratings of the units you're considering) in the event of an electrical power failure at your home.

VENTLESS (ALSO CALLED VENT-FREE) GAS FIREPLACES exhaust combustion byproducts directly into the room. They're slightly more efficient than direct-vent units and are even easier to install, but they deplete the room's oxygen supply and produce fumes that can be a health hazard. Some states have banned their use. Most of today's ventless gas fireplaces are required to include an oxygen depletion sensor (ODS), a safety feature that warns if oxygen levels in the room are becoming low. Still, for health reasons, you're much better off with a direct-vent appliance.

WOOD-BURNING STOVES are easier to install than wood-burning fireplaces. These airtight steel, cast iron, or stone units come in a variety of sizes and styles, including a range of rich colors. Many have a fireplace-like hearth and windowed doors that allow you to see the fire. They're a great backup heat source in the event of a power outage and burn quite efficiently (unlike wood-burning fireplaces, which generally suck heat out of the room and up the flue). Like the stove *below,* they require easy-to-install heat shields to protect the floor underneath them and the walls beside them. If you want a real wood-burning fireplace, these units offer a great combination of efficiency, durability, easy installation, and a variety of placement options. Plus, unlike built-in fireplaces, you can take them with you when you move, or use them in a different room in your house should your heating needs change.

WOOD-BURNING FIREPLACES that feature a firebox of heat-resistant metal don't require the additional floor support that masonry fireplaces do. These metal units can be surrounded by conventional wood framing and covered with drywall or a veneer of brick, stone, or other suitable material. In general most wood-burning fireplaces don't draw as well as a wood stove and can be smoky. They're also generally not as durable as a good-quality wood stove.

fitting in a bathroom

After you decide to locate a bathroom directly above, below, or back-to-back with the main plumbing stack, the next challenge is actually fitting in the toilet, sink, bath, and shower. Doing this in the basement isn't much different from doing it on a ground floor, though the closer you can locate the bathroom to the main drain line, the easier installing a branch drain (see page 146) will be. In the attic you may find yourself slipping a bathroom under a sloping ceiling or into tight quarters. The two attic spaces on these pages prove that full-service bathrooms can be achieved in the skinniest slivers of space.

Play the angles

When you're sitting in the tub, you don't need standing headroom . . . when you're standing at the shower, you do. The attic-eaves bath *below right* wisely places the tub's head end beneath the pitched ceiling's short wall and the shower-head along the tall wall. Similarly users need headroom arm's length from the vanity but not closer to it. The vanity *below left* stretches across a low dormer. A small mirror is mounted to the wall on a flexible arm, and the bather enjoys a great view and fresh breeze from a pretty window.

Three squares, one triangle

A random pattern of square tiles in three colors in a cream field lines the walls and floor to visually balance the strong triangular features in the bath *above*. Diagonally laid floor tiles seem to expand the space. A triangle-shape window fits the angles of the eaves *left*.

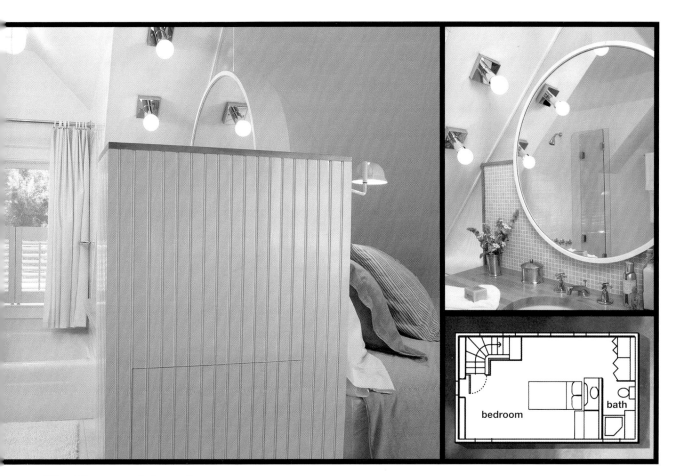

Bath and bed go back-to-back

Creating a bath-dressing corridor behind a built-in headboard provides the extra room necessary for a full bath in this pitched-roof attic suite. The vanity *above right* features a round two-sided mirror mounted to a tile backsplash half-wall. (On the sleeping side, the half-wall forms a beadboard headboard that's topped with the mirrored half-circle and fitted with two reading lamps.) A corner tub and shower with a glass door *above left* is tucked into a dormer.

Clearances and sizes for bathroom fixtures

The illustrations *right* provide an idea of how much space is needed for both bath fixtures and the clearance to use them. You're not limited to these, of course. If you have an odd-shape space, you can most likely find a fixture to fit it.

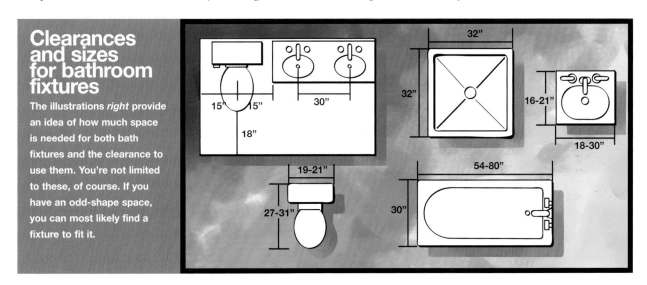

turn on the light

You're going to a lot of trouble to create a comfortable new living space, so you might as well do it right. You'll enjoy the room a lot more when it's fully and properly lit, so resist the temptation to put in a few overhead lights and leave it at that. A huge range of choices in lighting fixtures allows you to use them as an expression of your own style. So save room in the budget for some light sources that you'll enjoy.

AMBIENT LIGHT is the overall diffused light that comes from all of a room's light sources including its windows. Create ambient light with indirect light fixtures, such as sconces and torchères, which direct light upward, bouncing off the ceiling. In an attic small fixtures can be attached to rafter ties (if you have them) and directed upward. Lamps with open top shades also send light upward. Because ambient light contributes to a room's mood, put fixtures on dimmer switches (they cost a bit more than regular switches but are just as easy to install), so you're in control of the light level.

DOWNLIGHT is cast by ceiling fixtures, such as pendant, recessed, and track lights, and also by fluorescent light panels in suspended ceilings. As a rule, plan 1 incandescent watt per square foot of floor area when using a pendant or track light and 1.5 watts per square foot with a recessed can light. Don't forget to light the stairs. You need at least one 60-watt fixture per 10 feet of running stairs.

Fancy cover-up
Despite the attractive coffered ceiling treatment in this walk-out basement game room, ductwork and pipes hang as low as they do in ordinary basements—they're simply worked into the design. Recessed can lights illuminate the game table at night.

Plank top

Rough-sawn cedar planks make a fitting ceiling for the walk-out basement living space in this woodland home.

TASK LIGHTING illuminates a specific effort, whether it's reading in a chair, assembling a project at a counter, or playing a table game. Get this type of light from desk and table lamps, undercounter fixtures or strips, and ceiling- or wall-mounted spotlights. Light task settings with 150 watts of incandescent or 40 watts of fluorescent light. For long nights with a book, prevent eyestrain with 100 watts of incandescent or 30 watts of fluorescent light. Provide countertop and workshop activities with 120 watts of incandescent or 35 watts of fluorescent light for each 3 running feet of work surface.

ACCENT LIGHTING draws attention to great-looking room features. Use accent lights to spotlight a work of art, a tall plant, or wall texture. Find these lighting fixtures at the lighting store or home center; they're available in ceiling- and wall-mounted fixtures and also in portable plug-in models that you install according to changing needs.

Ceiling style

Attic ceilings are naturally dramatic, thanks to pitched rooflines, rafter ties, and dormers. Unlike basement ceilings they have no ductwork to conceal. You can cover an attic ceiling with beadboard, paneling, or ordinary painted drywall and you are guaranteed a pretty sight.

In the basement, though, unfinished ceilings are often low, and they bear a tangle of ductwork, wires, and pipes to work around.

ACOUSTIC TILES installed from a drop- or suspended-ceiling system are a low-cost, low-maintenance option. The system includes a framework of metal channels hung on wires attached to the joists. The channels support lightweight panels that form a finished surface.

DROP-CEILING SYSTEMS have had many critics in the past, but recent improvements have made them much more attractive and desirable. You won't have to move wires, pipes, or ducts to install the system, and joists don't have to be straight to achieve a finished ceiling that's flat and level. Gaining access to the heating, cooling, and electric systems is simply a matter of temporarily removing a panel. You can add lighting simply by removing a panel and fitting the opening with a drop-in fixture made for that purpose, or you can fit the panel with recessed can lighting.

DRYWALL is another option that results in a smooth, even finish that resembles a home's other living spaces. Drywall can be cut and shaped into coffered, tray, and other ceiling designs that are limited only by your imagination. Even if you choose wood paneling or some other surface for a ceiling, building code requires that a drywall base be installed first due to its fire-retardant quality.

Wiring, outlets, and switches

Save yourself the hassle of electric overloads by adding at least one general-purpose circuit to serve your newly remodeled space. If the space will have heavy electric demands, such as those in a woodworking shop, consider giving that room at least two circuits of its own. Likewise, give fixed appliances their own outlets and circuits.

■ Place an outlet on each wall longer than 2 feet.

■ Locate outlets so they're no more than 6 feet apart.

■ Install switches close to room entrances and exits.

■ Illuminate stairways with plenty of lighting, and install two-way switches at the top and bottom.

■ Install wiring for any cove, track, or other accent lighting you anticipate, even if you'll attach the fixtures later on.

Take some cues from retail settings

Retailers in many urban areas are as pressed for space as modern-day homeowners, and that often means heading for the basement—but it has got to look good! So when you're shopping in basement stores, keep your eyes open and notice how they make the space look so inviting. On these pages, take a look at how a home furnishings retailer makes an attractive place of its basement store—beautifully.

Texture makes things more interesting

White, light, and texture combine for backgrounds as airy and fresh as whipped cream. The look is a lovely complement to contemporary, country, or traditional-style furnishings. White-painted paneling *above* covers the ceiling and walls. Grooves in the paneling suggest there's something beyond, as if the room is a beach cabin and a breeze will be wafting through any moment. White floor-to-ceiling shutters

create interior windows that are lit from behind to suggest shards of infused sunlight. In the sitting area a dark armoire topped with a mirror forms a focal point. Dark furnishings add richness to a scheme that feels light overall.

Float the boundaries

The store defines spaces with floating room dividers: drywall panels covered with textural fabric, held in place with steel cables and turnbuckles screwed into the floor and ceiling *left*. Used in a home this technique allows free air circulation and floor-plan versatility.

Constructing a false lighted window

You can supplement natural light and create cheer in a dark area by including one or more false lighted windows in your below-grade space. Plan to use daylight spectrum fluorescent tubes; their light quality is much better than standard fluorescents. You may have to go to a lighting store and you'll pay a little more for them, but they're well worth the time and money. Here's how to make your window:

FRAME an interior window opening, as shown *below*.
INSTALL fluorescent light fixtures inside the window cavity horizontally, one at the top or two or three spaced evenly over the window opening.

WIRE FIXTURES to a light switch nearby.
INSTALL WINDOW TRIM PLUS QUARTER ROUND in the middle of the frame and around the window perimeter.
CUT FROSTED PLEXIGLASS to fit the window opening and set it in place against the quarter round.
CUT TWO MORE QUARTER-ROUND LENGTHS, press their flat side against the plexiglass and screw it into place. Fluorescent tubes are long-lasting and don't need to be changed often, but when they do, you'll need to unscrew and remove the quarter round.
DRESS THE WINDOW with sheer treatments (so the light shines through), such as shutters *opposite page* or a honeycomb blind topped with decorative panels *below*.

Sometimes the only thing that lies between your existing basement and a pleasing place to play, craft, or sleep is some quick and easy attention to walls, floor, and ceiling. The quick fixes here may provide all that you need to boost the appeal of your basement rooms. You also can use them as a bridge, making your basement more attractive while you phase in the more extensive remodeling work.

Take your walls undercover

A draping of fabric softens the look of boxy basement drywall or concrete block and hides cracks and imperfections indefinitely. Dewy apple-green check invigorates a bedroom *opposite*. The fabric is actually a series of top sheets; grommets are spaced evenly across the top edge of each sheet, which is hung from silver pegs mounted around the walls of the room. An obvious benefit of this wall treatment is that it can be changed in a flash to suit the season, inhabitant, or a whim. (This bedroom is also lightened with a faux window. For instructions on how to make one, see page 53.)

Up the style with steel and paint

For an instant contemporary look, buy panels of corrugated, galvanized steel and turn them into a decorative statement. Overlap the panels by two corrugations, pop-rivet them together, and screw them to studding (on interior walls) or over rigid foam panels and furring strips (on insulated exterior walls). Steel is sold at home centers in 8-foot by 2-foot, 2-inch panels (they're designed to be overlapped 2 inches, yielding 2-foot-wide panels when installed). You can bend panels around corners and overlap them, if necessary, reducing the need for cutting. If cutting is required, use a circular saw fitted with a metal cutting blade. Make smaller cuts for light switches and outlets with a saber saw or tin snips. An added benefit: The panels reflect light, brightening the space. For a similar but softer look, put up pale green or white corrugated plastic greenhouse roofing. Paint exposed floor joists, ductwork, and pipes to give them an architectural look. Install white track lighting directly on the joists, and your basement suddenly is a nicer place to be.

Floor moves

A concrete slab floor *below* becomes a lot more interesting with painted faux tiles, especially when the tiles are laid on the diagonal. First paint the entire floor with a high-quality, off-white, oil-based porch-and-deck enamel. Mask off grout lines of a width that suits you to create 12-, 15-, or 20-inch squares. Next roll on your tile color—a medium green was used on this floor—or get creative and use multicolored rag or sponge techniques to create the look you want. Finally, peel off the masking tape, revealing the faux grout lines. For added depth, gloss, and durability, top the whole floor with a couple of coats of high-quality clear floor finish.

Style on the quick and cheap

The basement space *below* was transformed in a weekend with coats of fresh white paint on block walls and corrugated, galvanized steel on an interior wall. The painted faux tiles over the concrete slab floor fool everyone.

Hang it up!

Sheets are a quick route to a fabric wall; they're already hemmed, and many come in coordinating prints. Have fun with your hanging hardware: Use pegs or attach ribbon loops to fabric and hang them over glass doorknobs or colorful shaped hardware.

Light and livable

By using one wall color for all basement-level spaces, including the office *above*, and divided light glass doors (not pictured), each room seems to flow into the next. Light bounces off the buttercream hue for a consistently sunny ambience. Several of the rooms feature false lighted windows (such as the one above the desk) that heighten the open, airy feel of the rooms even further.

Family flexibility

THE CHALLENGE: Drain and laundry hookups are installed in the ideal location for a family space.

THE SOLUTION: Relocate the drain and utility connections to a back room to free up space at the base of stairs for a room that serves family and friends.

THE SITUATION: A beautiful but cozy home in a great location combined with a growing family may necessitate developing your basement into a multipurpose family center. For best results, plan your changes in stages and set them in motion a few years before actually finishing (and desperately needing) the space. Be sure to install a sump pump for moisture control as well as egress windows for emergency exits. Section the floorspace into rooms that can be used for various purposes. The floor plan *below* shows five rooms: a main public room, utility room, office, and guest bedroom and bath. The main public room provides gathering space for families or an out-of-the-way playspace for children. The office provides dedicated space for a home business, and the guest suite makes room for frequent visitors. Close by but not interfering with living space, the utility room offers laundry and storage facilities.

LATER ON: The playroom can transform into a family computing or media center, home theater, or teen lounge. The office is large enough to accommodate two workstations, if needed. The bedroom and bath could serve as a teen suite or in-laws quarters.

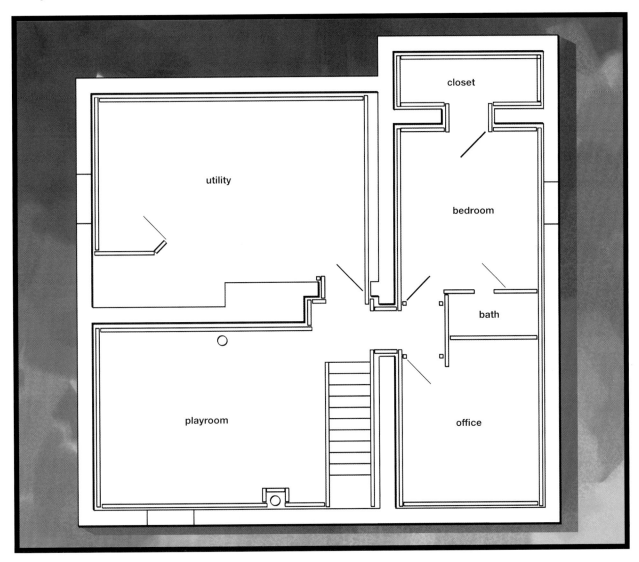

Now you see it, now you don't

See that mirror located at floor level on the block wall *above*? Behind it is a fireplace. When the fireplace is needed, a weighted pulley system raises the mirror on wall-mounted tracks. The fireplace is also open to the guest room behind it.

Floor plan labels: guest room · family room · hall · kitchen · wine storage

Party down

THE CHALLENGE: Create a sophisticated, large-scale entertaining area in a walk-out basement.

THE SOLUTION: A dramatic staircase (see floor plan *above* and photo on page 6) plus furniture groupings and floor coverings that define spaces in an open area.

THE SITUATION: A kitchen/bar and two conversation centers provide places to gather. A glass door displays the wine cellar and keeps its temperature just right. The fireplace serves both the sitting area and the guest room.

LATER ON: This floor plan has what it takes to become a comfortable apartment for in-laws.

A full suite below

THE CHALLENGE: Invigorate a big L-shape walk-out basement with architectural pizazz.

THE SOLUTION: Add an angled hallway, vibrant stained plywood walls, and glass-block wall accents.

THE SITUATION: A casual living and entertaining area, office/fitness spaces, dining/gaming space, and mini-kitchen replace a once cavernous, wide-open room. The spaces could have been dull but, with these decorative touches, a visually exciting amosphere emerged.

LATER ON: Thanks to a full bath and roomy closet, the office/workout space can easily convert into a guest suite.

Visual reward

Many thoughtful touches boost this basement's appeal. Walls of plywood marked off and stained with sheer colors garner interest; floor-to-ceiling slivers of glass block wall filter sparkling light; a shelving unit with blocklike geometry invites further inspection. Check out the floor plan: A faux lighted window hovers between the office and dining areas. (See page 53 for instructions on how to make one.)

Floor plan labels: closet, exercise/office, bar, bath, mech, family room, cleanout, sump pump, tv

Garage-top suite

THE CHALLENGE: Make a comfortable space for frequent houseguests who stay a while.

THE SOLUTION: Finish the bonus room over the garage; link it to the main house with an arbor-covered walk.

THE SITUATION: Big garages lead to big bonus rooms—the perfect location for an out-of-the-way guest suite. Light colors and a vaulted ceiling create an airy ambience. A kitchenette is composed of a single-basin sink, an undercounter refrigerator, cabinetry, and a toaster oven.

Opened up and linked

A shed dormer over the garage attic *below left* pops up from the roof to admit light and pretty views through a bank of three windows. Arbor-covered walks link the garage-top suite to the main house and a nearby smaller garage.

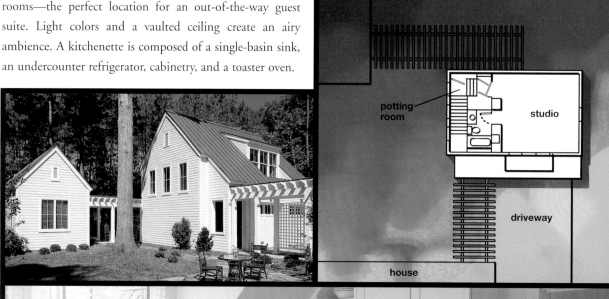

potting room

studio

driveway

house

Attic master suite

THE CHALLENGE: Double an attic's usable floor space.

THE SOLUTION: Put in a pair of 10-foot shed dormers.

THE SITUATION: To create a parent's dream getaway, one dormer makes room for a sleeping/sitting area; the other puts a roof over a hallway and double vanities. The tub, wall-free shower, and separate toilet area find room beneath the sloping ceiling. The dressing area with closets for two is part of an open hall that joins bed and bath.

LATER ON: The luxurious suite could accommodate a nanny or caregiver.

Sit for a bit

Topped with a cushion and fitted with a shelf below, a built-in bench beneath the windows *above* makes a handy resting spot and place to stash towels.

Multipurpose attic

THE CHALLENGE: Tray ceilings in second-floor rooms create uneven terrain upstairs.

THE SOLUTION: Use level variations and open railings to define spaces for different uses.

THE SITUATION: At the roofline a sitting area/media center and an office occupy opposite sides of the raised middle section. A roomy fitness room, complete with weight equipment, sits on one side of the office and sitting area; across from it an even larger, mirrored dance/aerobics room takes shape. A full bath, conveniently tucked under a dormer, rounds out the dance area end of the attic.

LATER ON: If desired this attic could easily become a guest suite; the dance room with bath could become an artist's studio with plenty of space for several to work.

For entrepreneurs the attic fitness area easily transforms into a large home office, and the raised office/sitting space becomes a family computing area.

Up and over

A raised, open room divides into two spaces with a passageway that joins a dance area and exercise room. A conversation/TV area sits to one side of the raised space, an office to the other. Neither area requires much headroom, which is reserved for the hallway that runs between them.

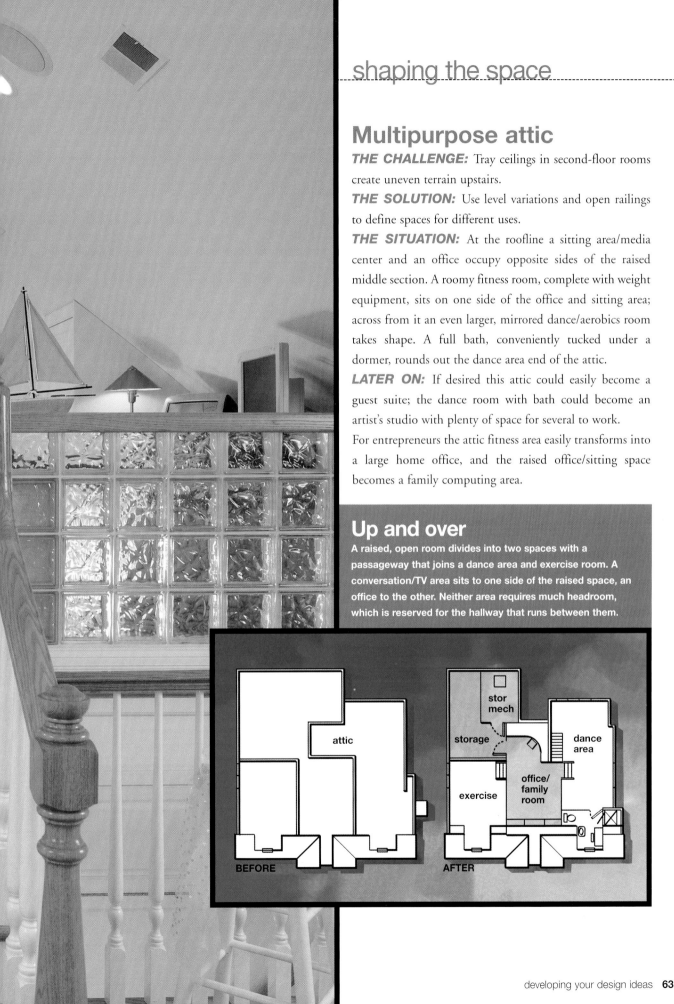

BEFORE

attic

AFTER

stor
mech

storage

dance area

office/ family room

exercise

While you're fiddling with your basement and attic floor plans, play with furnishing them too. Sketches of new space often give the impression that they have space to spare. But you want to make sure those new rooms can handle the functions—and each function's corresponding furnishings—that you have planned for them. Run your rough room sketches and space planning through the following steps.

MEASURE YOUR INTENDED ROOM. Plot it on a graph-paper grid with a scale of 1 square to 1 foot. Get a good start by tapping the "Room size recommendations" sidebar on page 39, but remember, they're guidelines.

FURNISH THE SPACE. Copy and cut out the furniture templates provided on pages 66–67, then place them in the intended spaces. Dab paper with a glue stick to keep furnishings in place on your sketch. Make your own templates for specialty pieces by measuring and drawing them to scale.

CREATE A FOCAL POINT. This is the physical cornerstone around which you arrange a furniture grouping. Visually a focal point is what draws you into a room and holds your attention. If your room doesn't have a natural focal point, such as a fireplace in the basement or a pretty attic window, create one. It can be an attractive media center, built-in bookcases with a nook for large pieces of art, or a large-scale piece of furniture, such as an armoire.

Remember the following tips when placing furniture in your room sketch:

DIRECT TRAFFIC STRATEGICALLY. Think of your furnishings as walls or guideposts that funnel traffic through each room. People passing through a room shouldn't break up a conversation grouping.

KEEP THINGS COZY. Try "floating" your furnishings by arranging them in such a way that people can visit with each other comfortably. In large spaces this generally means pulling furniture away from the walls into close groupings, with each piece of seating 8 feet or less from another piece. You also can float a piece away from the wall in smaller spaces, so conversation groupings stay tight and foot traffic is directed around the outside.

ARRANGE FOR CONVENIENCE. Provide a landing spot for drinks or books next to every seat. End tables, short

cabinets, and even an ottoman topped with a tray accomplish this task.

GO BOLD IN A SMALL ROOM. When you give a small room a large-scale attraction—whether it's a huge framed mirror or work of art—you give it grandeur.

FOOL THE EYE. Tall furniture and floor-to-ceiling cabinetry in a low-ceilinged room make a room appear taller. Underscore the drama with low seating pieces and low-positioned focal points for contrast.

Architectural symbols

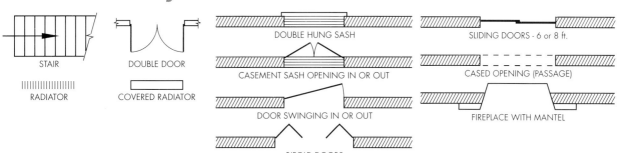

STAIR

RADIATOR

DOUBLE DOOR

COVERED RADIATOR

DOUBLE HUNG SASH

CASEMENT SASH OPENING IN OR OUT

DOOR SWINGING IN OR OUT

BIFOLD DOORS

SLIDING DOORS - 6 or 8 ft.

CASED OPENING (PASSAGE)

FIREPLACE WITH MANTEL

Make a strong focal point

In a box-shape basement room with no architectural highlights of its own, an attractive, lighted media center stands in as a focal point. The center's swooping, curved top and floating glass shelves attract attention and soften the room's boxy features. A set of recessed lights above highlight a selection of prints and pottery. The combination of the tall media center plus eye-level arrangement of poster, lamp, and low-back seating reduces the room's low-ceilinged feel.

Furniture templates

Find out what size, quantity, and arrangement of furnishings suit your new living spaces before you put hammer to nail. Photocopy and cut out these templates to furnish your rough floor plans. If everything you need doesn't fit, you can make adjustments or plan space-saving, double-duty solutions before you invest a penny in remodeling or furnishings. Make your own templates for furnishings not shown here using ¼-inch=1 foot graph paper and a scale of 1 foot: 1 square. Moving the sofa will never be easier.

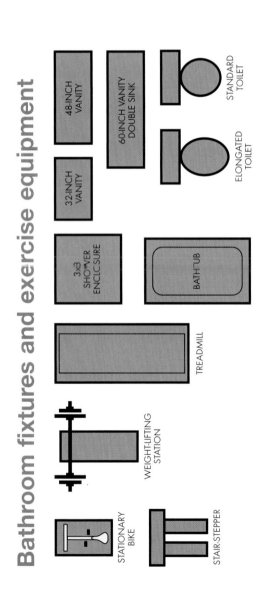

Bathroom fixtures and exercise equipment

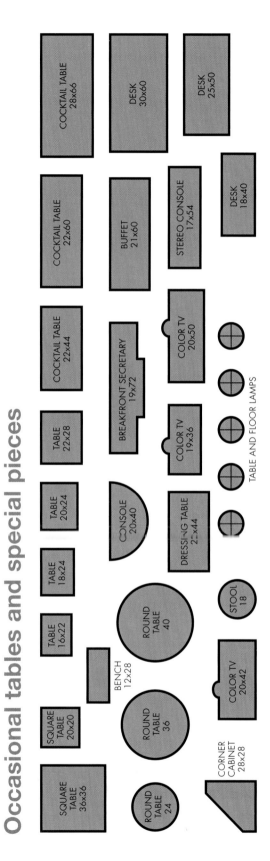

Occasional tables and special pieces

Dining room tables and chairs

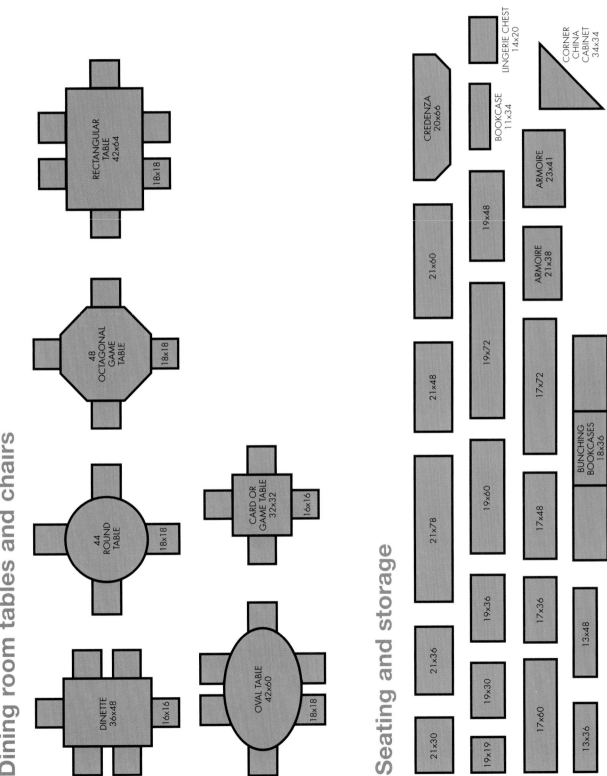

RECTANGULAR TABLE 42x64 — 18x18

OCTAGONAL GAME TABLE 48 — 18x18

ROUND TABLE 44 — 18x18

CARD OR GAME TABLE 32x32 — 16x16

DINETTE 36x48 — 16x16

OVAL TABLE 42x60 — 18x18

Seating and storage

CREDENZA 20x66

LINGERIE CHEST 14x20

BOOKCASE 11x34

CORNER CHINA CABINET 34x34

ARMOIRE 23x41

ARMOIRE 21x38

21x60

19x48

21x48

19x72

17x72

21x78

19x60

17x48

BUNCHING BOOKCASES 18x36

21x36

19x36

17x36

13x48

21x30

19x30

17x60

13x36

19x19

4

materials

AFTER YOU FIGURE OUT how you'd like to configure your new space it's time to choose the materials you'll use for construction and finishing. In this chapter you'll find an overview of material choices. Some, like 2×4 lumber and 4×8 sheets of drywall, are standard offerings that you'll be working with quite a bit, so it pays to know what's available and the functions for which each is designed. It also helps to know and understand what hardware and fasteners you need to assemble sturdy, high-quality floors, walls, and ceilings. Other materials—windows, skylights, climate-control appliances, and finish materials—offer another degree of choices. Read on to review the pros and cons of each so you can make selections that are ideal for your new space. Ready? Let's take a trip through the material world!

OPPOSITE: Black chalkboard paint creates a blank canvas that kids—and adults—can fill and refresh in this walk-out basement play/work space. Black outlet covers blend into the scheme. Crisp white beadboard on the lower walls sports trim broad enough to hold chalk and erasers. On the floor, tightly woven black olefin carpet is inset with a red-and-white checkerboard for game-playing fun.

Trim installation made easy

New high-tech trim options make it easier than ever to achieve an elegant look. Unlike the ornate (and often heavy) moldings of the past, which were painstakingly assembled from many carefully fitted pieces of wood, then painted and installed, the new high-tech moldings are made from light-weight urethane foam. Some even come with miterless corners, eliminating the need to cut precision mortars or cope cuts, and making installation all the easier.

Framing lumber makes up the skeleton of walls. You will use mostly 2×4s and 2×6s. Occasionally you may need something wider, such as a 2×8, a 2×10, or even a 2×12. On the wider pieces (2×8, 2×10, 2×12), the actual width is about ¾ inch narrower than the nominal width; on the smaller pieces, the actual width is ½ inch less.

Grade

Many home centers stock two or more grades of lumber; the lower the grade number, the higher the quality. If the lumber will be covered by other materials, you generally can get by with a lower, less-expensive grade of wood, such as grade 2 or 3, especially if you have the opportunity to hand-pick each piece of wood. Eliminate those that are cracked, warped, have wane (are not the full dimension for the full length of the board), bark, loose knots (knots encirlced with bark) or several large knots.

Lengths

Most framing lumber comes in 8-foot and greater lengths, increasing in 2-foot increments. Keep lengths in mind as you make your shopping list; you may be able to cut a single long piece into the shorter pieces you need. Many suppliers also stock what they call precut studs. These are 2×4s that are 91½ inches long, the right size for 8-foot walls (double top and single bottom plates add 4½ inches to the overall wall height).

Trim

Generally made of solid softwood such as fir or pine, but occasionally available in oak or other woods, trim is thinner than framing lumber and serves a decorative function. Trim comes in two grades.

STAIN-GRADE moldings are cut from long, knot-free lengths of wood and are meant to be finished with stain, a clear wood finish, or both.

PAINT-GRADE OR FINGER-JOINTED moldings are usually cheaper than stain-grade moldings, and are made of short sections of wood joined end to end. Paint-grade moldings made up of medium-density fiberboard (MDF) are also available. Some larger, more ornate crown moldings are made of urethane foam. These synthetic moldings cost much less than their wooden counterparts, are easy to install, and take paint beautifully.

Trim types

Many rooms feature baseboard and crown molding; others are embellished with more. Consider using the following:

CASING is applied around door and window frames.

BASEBOARD serves as a transition between the bottom of the wall and the floor.

CROWN MOLDING embellishes the intersection of the wall and ceiling.

CHAIR RAIL keeps the backs of chairs from marring walls; it's generally fastened to the wall about 3 feet off the floor.

PICTURE-FRAME MOLDING offers a sturdy surface from which to hang pictures; it's usually mounted about 26 inches down from the ceiling.

Sheet stock

These products are sold in 4×8-foot sheets in thicknesses that range from 1/8 inch to 1 1/4 inches (although the thickest and the thinnest sizes may be harder to find.) You typically can buy quarter and half sheets as well. Although the oldest and best known of these products is plywood, there are other varieties as well, each with its own special properties. Here's an overview of what's available and their common uses:

PLYWOOD is a sandwich of thin layers of wood called plies or veneers. Each successive ply is laid with its grain running at 90 degrees to the previous layer. The resulting sheet is very strong and stable. Construction plywood is made of softwood veneers and graded according to the quality of the veneers that make up the two outside faces. These grades are, from best to worst, A, B, C, and D. Higher grades are sanded smooth with knots, holes, and imperfections filled; lower grades are progressively rougher and less uniform.

MEDIUM-DENSITY FIBERBOARD (MDF) is made of fine wood fibers that have been pressed and glued together. The resulting sheets are very smooth and flat. MDF takes paint well and is a good choice for interior shelving and painted cabinetry.

PARTICLEBOARD, made of coarser wood particles than those used to make MDF, is commonly used as a floor underlayment and as the bottom layer for countertops.

ORIENTED STRAND BOARD (OSB), made of even bigger pieces of wood, is stronger than either MDF or particleboard, though not as strong as plywood. It is commonly used for sheathing and roof decking.

Fasteners

You'll find hundreds of different types of fasteners. Most interior remodeling projects, however, need only the following:

NAILS FOR FRAMING

The job of framing requires **COMMON NAILS**—those with smooth shanks for easy driving and big heads for lots of holding power.

16D COMMON NAILS (3 1/2 inches long) attach studs (vertical pieces of lumber) to plates (horizontal pieces) and anchor plates to the floor.

10D COMMON NAILS (3 inches long) are good for general nailing, such as fastening two studs face-to-face.

8D COMMON NAILS (2 1/2 inches long) are good for toe-nailing at an angle through one piece of wood into the face of another piece.

NAILS FOR INSTALLING SHEET STOCK

For easy finishing and increased holding power, use the following specialty nails when appropriate:

DRYWALL NAILS have slightly cupped heads that dent the surface of the drywall and allow them to be more easily concealed by drywall compound.

RINGSHANK, CONCRETE-COATED, AND SPIRAL-SHANK NAILS have increased holding power for installing plywood, OSB subflooring, and underlayment.

NAILS FOR INSTALLING TRIM AND DOORS

For attaching trim and hanging doors, you need **FINISH NAILS** or **CASING NAILS.** Both types of fasteners have a small head that allows you to drive them below the surface of the wood and hide them from view with dabs of wood putty. A supply of **4D, 6D, 8D,** and **16D** finish or casing nails handles any finish trim job you may encounter.

SCREWS

These familiar fasteners have threads that bite into wood fibers, and thus have greater holding power than nails of a similar size. They're also easier to remove without damaging the materials they fasten, a handy trait if you're constructing something that will be disassembled later, such as a temporary support wall. With the advent of the power drill/driver, bugle-head screws, such as *DRYWALL SCREWS,* which are generally black and threaded from the head to their sharply pointed ends, or *DECK SCREWS,* which are rustproof and have somewhat coarser threads and thicker shanks for holding larger framing, have replaced traditional wood screws. These fasteners don't require the drilling of pilot holes for most applications. They're strong, hold well, and install quickly.

For the job of hanging drywall, you need *1¼-INCH* screws. Have some *1⅝-INCH, 2-INCH, 2½-INCH,* and *3-INCH* screws on hand for general use.

FRAMING CONNECTORS

Each of these inexpensive, galvanized, stamped-steel devices is designed for a special purpose.

JOIST HANGERS simplify joist installation and make the plank stronger.

RAFTER TIES connect rafters to top plates.

TENSION BRIDGES add lateral strength to floor and ceiling joists.

ANGLE BRACKETS add strength to perpendicular joints (at rim joists and stair stringers, for example).

MASONRY FASTENERS

Some masonry fasteners are hard enough to be hammered directly into concrete; others expand to grip the inside of a hole you drill into the masonry using a power drill and a masonry bit.

MASONRY NAILS are made of hardened steel with squared edges and a rough surface that grips concrete.

ANCHOR BOLTS have a band at the base that expands when you tighten the bolt. Use them to fasten framing members to concrete walls or slabs.

EXPANSION SHIELDS slip into holes that have been drilled into the masonry. The metal shields expand, gripping the hole when a screw is driven in.

WALL ANCHORS are similar to expansion shields, with flanges, toggles, or flaring plastic tips that grip the interior surface of the mounting hole.

Adhesives and fillers

In addition to mechanical fasteners, numerous chemical adhesives and fillers on the market help you stick things together and create a smooth finish. Here are a few of the most common:

CONSTRUCTION ADHESIVE fastens a wide variety of materials together; it's often used to adhere drywall or paneling to framing. It comes in tubes and is dispensed with a caulking gun.

YELLOW WOOD GLUE is sometimes used to install moldings and other trim.

JOINT COMPOUND OR DRYWALL MUD is used for filling the seams and covering screw or nail holes in drywall. It is commonly sold in 5-gallon buckets, though smaller quantities are available.

CAULK is used for disguising gaps in moldings. It also comes in tubes.

CELLULOSE-FIBER WOOD FILLER is the material of choice for hiding nailheads in trim. If you are staining the trim, wood filler is available in colors to match.

WAX CRAYON WOOD FILLER, available in a variety of colors, is also used to hide nailheads in trim. Apply the filler after the first coat of clear finish.

Wall materials

Drywall is the ubiquitous choice, although sheet paneling options have increased dramatically in recent years, and tongue-and-groove paneling remains popular also.

DRYWALL

The wall surface in most houses today is called drywall, a thick layer of gypsum sandwiched between two layers of paper. Drywall is inexpensive, fire-resistant, and sound-absorbing. It's sold in sheets that are 4 feet wide and 8 to 16 feet long. The long edges of the sheets are tapered to make an easier job of creating a flat seam where two pieces adjoin.

You can embellish drywall with paint, paneling, wallpaper, moldings—just about any decorative treatment you can imagine—and install and finish it with common and relatively inexpensive tools. Disadvantages to using drywall include the fact that the sheets are heavy and awkward to transport and handle. Also mudding, taping, and sanding joints takes some practice to master and is a dusty, messy, and time-consuming process.

Here are your drywall choices and the applications best for each type:

¼-INCH makes gentle bends and is good for covering curved surfaces.

⅜-INCH is used for covering existing walls.

½-INCH is used for most wall and ceiling installations.

⅝-INCH is more fire resistant than thinner sheets and is used often where extra fire resistance is specified, such as on a wall between an attached garage and a house. It also is stiffer than the thinner sheets, so it makes for flatter walls and better sound absorption.

MOISTURE-RESISTANT (also called green board due to the color of its paper facing) is meant for use in damp locations, such as bathrooms and laundry rooms. It is somewhat more flexible than regular drywall and tends to sag, especially when damp. For this reason it must be fastened every 12 inches when used for ceilings rather than the typical 16-inch spacing.

SHEET PANELING

Made of either hardboard or thin plywood with a decorative facing, sheet paneling is available in an assortment of looks. These include real-wood veneers, such as maple, birch, and pickled finishes, as well as traditional mahogany, oak, pine, and cedar. Some panels, such as beadboard, are available pre-painted—a design plus if you're going for the casual cottage or farmhouse look. Some paneling also is available unfinished so you can stain or paint them to suit your decorating scheme. Water-resistant melamine finishes that mimic tile, complete with embossed grout lines, are available at a much lower cost than a real tile wall. Some varieties of sheet paneling even look like wallpaper or offer surprisingly realistic photo reproductions of exotic wood species. Sheet paneling

is relatively inexpensive and, because the 4×8 sheets are relatively lightweight and require no messy taping, mudding, and sanding, they go up fast.

TONGUE-AND-GROOVE WOOD PANELING

These planks are available in pine, redwood, cedar, oak, and mahogany, to name only the most popular species. Some styles come in planks with vertical grooves that give it the look of several narrower strips. Some planks are prefinished; some are unfinished. Because the planks are solid wood, the paneling is heavier and more expensive (per square foot of installed wall) than sheet paneling. It also takes more time to hang, though the installation process is not difficult.

Flooring materials

A properly prepared basement, attic, or bonus room floor can benefit from virtually the same wide range of flooring choices available to the rest of your home. Some of the most popular options follow.

CARPET is warm, inviting, and quiet and comfortable underfoot. It is available in a range of colors and textures and doesn't require you to be as fussy about the condition of the underlayment as are some other flooring options, although you may want to hire a professional to install it. Combined with a good-quality pad, carpet is effective at muffling sounds—an especially important consideration in an attic remodel where rooms are located over bedrooms. You can use carpet in a basement as well, provided the space has been waterproofed and the floor well-prepared (see pages 145–148).

HARDWOOD is beautiful, durable, and complements a host of interior design schemes. You'll find dozens of species, finishes, and configurations available, including nail-down strip planks, parquet squares, self-stick squares and planks, and prefinished options, many of which you can easily install yourself. A downside: Wood is a hard surface that offers little cushioning and sound absorption, so you may want to use throw rugs or area rugs to limit noise and provide a softer surface in high-traffic areas.

LAMINATE offers the look of wood and other natural materials at a lower price. Available in strips or tiles, laminate is durable and easy-to-clean, installs easily, is highly impact-

Furniture for your floor

Above: Properly prepared, basement and attic floors can be finished quite beautifully. This floor *above*, finished in an elegant, clear-finished cherry hardwood, makes a great backdrop for clean-lined, contemporary furnishings. Other traditional choices include tile, laminate, vinyl, and carpet.

resistant, and requires little maintenance. Keep in mind that it can't be refinished or restained like wood.

CERAMIC TILE comes in a variety of sizes and colors that allow you to create exciting patterns. It is durable, resistant to moisture, and generally low-maintenance. On the down-side, ceramic tile can feel cold, is unforgiving, and can be uncomfortable to stand on for long periods of time. Also dirt can collect in the grout lines.

VINYL, available as sheet goods and tiles (including easy-to-install, self-stick tiles), is a good-looking, low-cost, and easy-care choice, although it requires a smooth and level underlayment. You'll find an enormous selection of colors and styles, including well-designed wood, tile, and stone look-alikes. Vinyl tiles can eventually loosen and admit moisture and dirt; less expensive grades sometimes puncture, fade, and discolor quickly. It's worth the extra expense to buy a higher-quality product.

LINOLEUM is made primarily of natural materials. It is soft underfoot, comes in both tiles and sheets of solid or flecked colors, and is very durable. It does require periodic maintenance and professional installation.

CORK provides a resilient, cushioned surface that is noise-less, comfortable, and moisture-resistant. Made from renewable bark that's harvested from cork oak trees in Mediterranean forests, cork requires a urethane finish (some varieties are finished in the factory) to facilitate sweeping and mopping. Sand the old finish and reapply new urethane every few years, and cork flooring can last for decades.

BAMBOO may look like hardwood, but it's actually three layers of grass that have been laminated under high pressure to create planks. Three coats of acrylic urethane render the surface durable and resistant to water, mildew, and insect damage. Harder than maple and oak, bamboo also expands and contracts less than hardwoods, so it's a somewhat better choice if your renovated space will be exposed to variations in temperature and humidity.

PAINT offers a low-cost alternative that you can apply directly to a subfloor or bare concrete floor, provided the floor is clean, smooth, free of defects, and all screw and nail-heads are flush or driven below the surrounding surfaces. Decorative paint techniques such as stenciling are fun do-it-yourself projects (see "Floor moves" on page 54).

Unfinished attics and basements rarely have the means to let in enough daylight and ventilation for living areas, so you probably want to install windows (and/or skylights if you're remodeling attic spaces) as part of your plan. Here's an overview of what's available:

Window types

Windows are available to suit nearly any style of architecture. Choose those that blend with the other windows of your house, especially if you're installing them in a location that is prominent when viewed from the outside.

DOUBLE-HUNG AND SINGLE-HUNG These traditional designs are still the most common. Double-hung windows feature a pair of movable sashes that slide vertically within the window frame. Single-hung models also feature an upper and lower sash; only the lower sash is operative.

CASEMENT These windows pivot on hinges as doors do, but they usually swing outward and are controlled by a hand-crank mechanism affixed to the windowsill. Casement shapes tend toward the tall and narrow, so wide wall openings usually feature multiples, sometimes with a fixed picture window in the center. Ventilation is generous relative to

Let there be light

You're not limited to the small basement windows most builders install. Cut into the wall *above* and you can install full-size windows for lots of light and air.

Same window, three looks

A basic double-hung window takes on different personalities, depending on its muntins and trim. From left to right, the windows *below* are at home in colonial, contemporary, and Mission-style architecture.

Special features

A variety of details can make your new windows easier to live with.

TILTING SASHES Many double-hung windows now come with tilting sashes, *below,* so both interior and exterior glass surfaces can be cleaned from the inside of the house—an especially useful feature on second-story windows.

DETACHABLE GRILLES Muntin and grille options do a good job of mimicking the look of a true divided-light window, in which small individual panes of glass are separated by the muntin framework. Snap-on grilles are the most affordable option. They attach to the inside and/or outside of the sash and can be removed easily to clean the glass. Simulated divided-light windows feature both of these surface-mounted grilles and also have a matching grid sandwiched between the panes of glass for a more authentic look. Look for the kind that snap on and off easily and without tools to speed window washing.

IMPROVED CRANK HARDWARE Some manufacturers offer collapsible or low-profile handles for crank-out windows, such as casements and awnings. These don't interfere with the drop of blinds or other window coverings.

LOCK-AND-LATCH OPTIONS A variety of materials, finishes, and types are available to match your decor and ensure your security.

BETWEEN-PANE FEATURES Some windows feature built-in miniblinds or pleated shades that drop down between the panes, where they stow out of the way when raised and never need dusting.

overall window area because the entire sash swings open, but exposure of the outward-swinging frame can be a problem if rain arrives suddenly. Because many casements don't meet code requirements for egress windows (those that provide passage in case of fire), they're not often used in bedrooms.

AWNING This is another type of hinged window, but one that pivots at the top. With their horizontal rather than vertical orientation, awnings don't open as fully as casements but offer the advantage of shedding water harmlessly if left open during a rainfall. Although they can be used alone, they're often installed above or below large picture windows to provide ventilation at the top or bottom of a wall. They also face limitations in meeting egress code requirements for use as bedroom windows.

GLIDING In a gliding window one or two sashes slide horizontally in the tracks of the window frame. Gliders used to have a strong horizontal orientation, so they often worked best with home designs, such as ranches or Prairie-style buildings that have strong horizontal lines. Nowadays, vertical sliders are also available.

PICTURE These stationary windows provide light and views only. When maximum views are the objective, picture windows offer the least obstruction. Ventilation requirements are often handled by installing operative windows above, below, or alongside a picture window.

Window glazing options

The type of glazing you want depends on the location and application of the window. Paying extra for low-E glass on unshaded windows that face south makes perfect sense and is a good investment, but paying extra doesn't make sense for windows that are shaded or face north.

DOUBLE-PANE GLASS With a few exceptions for southern regions and economy-grade product lines, virtually all good-quality windows manufactured today are fitted with insulated glass. This means the glazing is actually a sandwich of two panes of glass separated by warm channel spacers. The spacers act as thermal breaks to keep the exchange of inside and outside temperatures to a minimum. Double-pane glass is twice as efficient as single-pane.

TRIPLE-PANE GLASS has three panes; it's three times

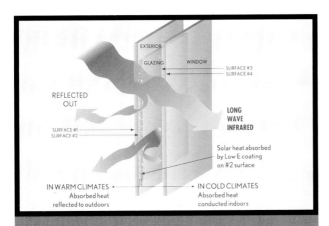

Anatomy of a window

A double-glazed, low-E window features a metallic coating on the inside of the exterior pane that reflects heat in warm climates and absorbs it in cold climates.

more energy-efficient than single-pane glass.

ARGON-FILLED GLASS uses argon instead of air between two panes of glass. These panes provide an energy efficiency similar to triple-pane glass, but they weigh less, so they're easier to open and close. (Unless you are ordering custom windows, the units you buy will be dual-glazed and argon-filled.)

LOW-E GLASS Many manufacturers offer low-E glass (for low emissivity), which is coated with a microscopic layer of silver and metal oxides. It permits 75 percent of visible light to pass through but reduces heat transfer, helping to keep houses warmer in winter and cooler in summer. Low-E glass also blocks infrared and most ultraviolet light, thereby reducing fading.

HIGH-STRENGTH GLASS Two types of high-strength glass are available. Tempered glass is required by code for certain applications, such as glass doors and window installations with low sill heights. For more extreme conditions, such as coastal environments, consider laminated, impact-resistant glass designed to withstand hurricane-force winds and the impact of airborne debris.

Window frame options

Attic windows, in particular, can be difficult—if not downright dangerous—to access for periodic scraping and painting. Make low-maintenance materials a high priority when buying those windows.

WOOD It's the traditional, and most common, material for jambs, sash frames, sills, and trim, and it's still available. With proper care, wood-framed windows look good and perform reasonably well because wood is a fairly good insulator. Wood frames require periodic maintenance to prevent water and sun damage, however, and they sometimes shrink and warp, resulting in drafts. These days, about 90 percent of wood-framed windows sold are clad, or wrapped outside with a weatherproof covering, to eliminate the need for painting and to protect the structure of the window from the elements. Choose color wisely. Although they can be painted, if you do so, you'll be stuck with the same periodic maintenance that you'd have with unclad windows. The interior surfaces can be stained or painted.

WOOD COMPOSITE Recently wood composites (a mix of shredded wood fiber and plastic resins) have become more common for the structural core of window frames and components. These compounds are extruded into hollow tube shapes, then covered with a vinyl or aluminum-cladding exterior and a paint primer or vinyl-cladding interior. This approach capitalizes on the strength and insulating properties of wood but doesn't require the expensive high-grade materials used in solid-wood frames. They save you money, but you can't use a transparent stain on interior surfaces.

VINYL CLADDING Vinyl has excellent impact resistance and integral color, so scratches on the surface don't expose the layer underneath. Vinyl-clad windows are available in a

Energy efficiency made easy

Look for the following when buying windows. In each case the lower the value, the more energy-efficient the window: **U-VALUES** The National Fenestration Rating Council (NFRC) rates the windows of participating manufacturers for the amount of heat that flows through a product (its U-value). **SOLAR HEAT GAIN COEFFICIENCY (SHGC)** reflects the amount of energy that passes from the exterior to the interior, and air leakage.
ENERGY STAR To quickly identify good performers, the Energy Star program, a voluntary partnership between the U.S. Department of Energy and participating manufacturers, gives its seal of approval to windows with a U-value of 0.35 or lower, and an SHGC rating of 0.40 or lower.

Attic windows

When you are planning and sizing windows for attic end walls, keep these points in mind:

AIM FOR EYE LEVEL OR ABOVE. Windows that are too low to see the horizon create uncomfortable viewing angles; windows placed higher than eye level are fine—they gather interesting views of the sky and afford both natural light and privacy.

KEEP SILLS AT LEAST 2 FEET OFF THE FLOOR. Lower sills can be a safety hazard for children or pets who may run into them.

COORDINATE FURNISHINGS WITH WINDOW PLACEMENT. You don't want to end up putting a tall chest of drawers or other large piece of furniture in front of a window or placing reading chairs across the room and away from the light.

LOOK AT WINDOW PLACEMENT FROM THE OUTSIDE TOO. The style and placement of your windows should be in harmony with your home's architecture.

ture. Some manufacturers use steel inserts to add strength and stiffness to the frames—a feature you can request. But only time will tell how these windows—a relatively recent

Impact-resistant glass

If you live in a hurricane-prone area, consider impact-resistant glass, which is designed to prevent flying debris from penetrating windows. The 2×4 *below* was fired at the window from a cannon; it didn't penetrate.

limited number of color choices, usually white, dark taupe or neutral brown, and light, neutral beige.

ALUMINUM CLADDING Aluminum requires more care in handling to avoid scratches or dents, but the factory-applied paint finishes are extremely durable and typically come in several colors.

ALUMINUM FRAMES Less expensive than wood and clad-wood frames, uninsulated aluminum frames are also low-maintenance, whether you choose the silver, unpainted mill finish, or factory-applied painted finishes. Although they perform well in warmer regions, aluminum is a poor insulator, and energy losses combined with condensation and the frost that forms on the interior of aluminum frames in cold weather make these windows a poor choice for colder regions.

FIBERGLASS FRAMES Fiberglass combines the high stability and strength of aluminum with the insulating properties of wood and vinyl. Fiberglass frames usually cost more than frames made of wood and vinyl. Some manufacturers combine fiberglass exteriors with wood interiors, a hybrid approach that combines low maintenance with reasonable cost.

VINYL FRAMES These relatively low-cost frames offer low maintenance and good insulation but lack the structural rigidity of either wood or aluminum. The frames flex more, and they also move in response to swings in tempera-

addition to the market—hold up over the long haul. Attics and basements face opposite environmental extremes when it comes to climate control.

BASEMENTS are typically cool year-round—comfortably so in summer, a bit chilly in winter. Often basements are partially insulated by the ground around them so the amount of heat they need to bring them up to habitable temperatures is usually moderate and can be handled by the existing heating system. Many basements in homes heated by forced hot air already have the necessary ductwork. If not, a technician can install ductwork relatively simply and inexpensively because a furnace is generally located on that level. Still, your basement may need a supplemental heat source. If you have a walk-out basement with large, unshaded, south-facing windows, you may need supplemental cooling as well.

ATTICS, on the other hand, are typically easier to heat than to cool because hot air rises. Their exposed locations usually require some heating during winter and considerable cooling during summer. Attics are harder to tie into existing climate-control systems because they are so far from the furnace and air-conditioning unit. And the unit may not have enough capacity—especially air-conditioning capacity—to do the job. Consult a qualified Heating, Ventilation, and Air-Conditioning (HVAC) technician before you remodel.

Keeping warm

If modifying or expanding the main HVAC system in your home is impractical, you still have options. In fact some of the products listed below may prove more efficient, especially if your new space will not be in constant use.

ELECTRIC HEATERS are generally the easiest and cheapest to install but the most expensive to operate. Electric heat can be an efficient and comfortable solution, however, if you live in a mild climate, heat only sporadically, and/or heat only a small area.

BASEBOARD HEATERS come in lengths of 4 or 6 feet and operate on normal household electrical current. Plug them into a wall outlet or hard-wire them to an electrical circuit. Baseboard heaters are quiet and easy to conceal, but again, more costly and ineffective in larger areas.

ELECTRIC WALL HEATERS have built-in fans to dis-

Skylights

A skylight is the best source for direct natural light. Once considered a luxury, today's products are affordable and available in a broad range of styles, from simple plastic bubbles to those with electrically driven openers and shading devices. The job of installing a skylight may seem like a daunting task but, with basic carpentry skills, the right tools, and clear instructions, you can enjoy a new skylight that's not only beautiful but trouble-free. Skylights are available with many of the same glazing, frame, cladding, and special features available to other windows, but a few additional details pertain to skylights:

SQUARE OR RECTANGULAR skylights have either wood or metal frames. Bubble-type skylights are always plastic, but flat glazing may be plastic or glass.

OPERABLE SKYLIGHTS open; fixed skylights don't.

ROOF WINDOWS, a variation of a skylight, are designed to be installed at eye level, often in a steeply pitched roof. They're ideal for attic remodelings. Some can be opened by remote control.

SPECIALTY SKYLIGHTS can be ordered with interior or exterior awnings, bronze and gray-tinted glass, low-E reflective coatings, and gas-filled double-pane glazing to help mitigate heat gain or loss and the fading effect of direct sunlight. Some plastic skylights are available with a bronze tint; a light-diffusing, white plastic surface; or a honeycomb material specially designed to diffuse light evenly and provide insulation against heat loss and gain.

TUBULAR SKYLIGHTS *below* are a relatively recent and effective innovation that feature a top with a domed lens, a tubular shaft coated with a light-reflective material, and a diffuser on the shaft bottom. The tube is mounted flush with the room ceiling, spreading light into the room below. Some come with a light kit, providing the option of an electric light fixture that can be switched on after the sun goes down.

Warm the room with a gas fireplace

Gas fireplaces are ideal for basement and attic conversions that need a source of additional heat on occasion. The fireplaces install easily, are energy-efficient, and offer ambience along with warmth.

tribute heat and are small enough to fit in confined spaces, such as bathrooms and knee walls. Because of their fans wall heaters distribute heat faster but make somewhat more noise. They also must be hard-wired into your home's circuits. Consider furniture placement when you locate a wall heater; you want to avoid blocking the fan.

PORTABLE HEATERS come in several varieties: radiant heaters, which produce instant warmth; oil-filled radiators, which produce a quiet, even heat; and ceramic heaters, which are powerful yet compact. These heaters allow you to heat just the area you're using and are an efficient way to keep comfortable if you don't use your new space for long periods of time. The newest ceramic heaters, which use an electronic temperature control to smoothly vary the output

of both the heating element and a very quiet fan, are particularly impressive for their small size and ability to hold a constant temperature without cycling on and off.

GAS HEATERS are a more efficient choice if your space is large and/or used often. More expensive and more work to install than electric heaters, these units are quiet, powerful, and efficient. Products are made to run on either natural gas or bottled LP gas; buy the correct type for the fuel you have available. Have these heaters professionally installed.

DIRECT-VENT GAS HEATERS are efficient, quiet, thermostatically controlled units that provide abundant, clean heat. They're designed to heat a room's air and then distribute the heated air with a fan. A pipe that exits the rear of the appliance penetrates an exterior wall, vents exhaust gases, and draws combustion air into the appliance.

DIRECT-VENT GAS FIREPLACES are a bit more complex to install than gas heaters, but they allow you to see the flames and be warmed by their radiant heat. Some include a fan to distribute warmed air as well, making them efficient as well as decorative. See page 47 for a more thorough discussion of these products.

WOOD HEAT from most wood-burning fireplaces sucks more hot air out of a room than it produces, so these fireplaces are mostly decorative and ambience-enhancing. But air-tight, wood-burning stoves, some of which allow you to view the fire, can be a great way to heat your new space, especially if you have a good source of wood to burn. They require lighting, stoking, ash-cleaning, and the carrying in and out of messy fuel, though, so they're not for everyone. See page 47 for a more thorough discussion.

Staying cool

Fortunately, the chief disadvantage of an attic—summer heat—is easy to deal with, especially if you insulate the roof as part of your remodeling project.

WINDOW AIR-CONDITIONERS are good at providing supplemental cooling. If you haven't bought one in a while, you'll be pleased at how much quieter and more efficient the new units are. Before purchasing a window unit, measure the square footage of your rooms. Window units generally include ratings that indicate the square footage they can effectively cool. Don't buy too large a unit and expect better performance—while an oversize unit will initially cool down the room faster, it won't dehumidify the room nearly as well

as a properly sized unit, and it will use more energy too. Place these units in a window or in an opening created just for them—so they won't obstruct daylight or views—and always install them securely.

PORTABLE AIR-CONDITIONERS are about the same size and shape as portable dehumidifiers. They're on wheels, so you can move them to just the area you need to cool. A flexible hose vents the hot exhaust to the outside, usually through a window kit that you install by simply opening a nearby window a few inches and fitting the adjustable kit in the space between the sash and the sill. Similar to a dehumidifier, condensed water accumulates in a slide-in bucket that you empty periodically. While more expensive than a window unit of comparable capacity, these coolers are a great solution if true portability is what you're after.

Wood stoves

Air-tight, wood-burning stoves, such as this porcelain-glazed cast iron model, are an efficient and abundant source of heat.

5

fine-tuning your plan

IN THIS TRANSITIONAL PHASE visions of your transformed basement, attic, or bonus room are becoming increasingly clear. Sketches fill your notebooks and you can visualize how you're going to use your new space in great detail. You've been working on a basic floor plan and even know what kinds of materials you'd like to use. Now is the time to fine-tune your plans. That means drawing your plans more fully, deciding just how you'll gain that floor space in the attic, and making room for supporting features such as storage. It also means deciding exactly what you'll include in your new space—a television, refrigerator, or sink—and where you'll connect those amenities to utilities.

With your plans completed it's time to figure how the work will get done. That means creating a budget for yourself and sizing up what you'll do, and what you'll hire others to do. Your ideas are one step away from becoming a reality.

OPPOSITE: An attic knee wall becomes the focal point of a seating area when it's fitted with a ventilated television cabinet and flanked by display cabinets with glass-fronted doors. Notice the cabinet trim: Fluorescent tubes are tucked behind it for soft uplighting.

When your basement, attic, or bonus room plans are final, make some drawings of what the new space will look like: A basic bird's-eye view (architects call this a "plan view") will serve as the lead drawing. Other drawings detail your framing, plumbing, and electrical plans, and provide constant references as you purchase materials and work the space. When drawing your plan view, plot the location of features along each wall, including jogs, windows, stairs, doors, outlets, and switches. Mark the location of all utilities and connections, drains, pumps, and any fixed features, such as steel posts. Use a dotted line to indicate any feature that affects the space from above, such as a skylight; use a different color to indicate features you'll be removing, such as a wall.

Measuring tips

Note all measurements in inches.

MARK THE NORTHWEST CORNER of the space with a star. Begin measuring from this corner.

MEASURE FROM THE NORTHWEST CORNER to the first jog, opening, window, or door on the first (north) wall, proceeding around the space in a clockwise direction.

MEASURE THE WIDTH OF ANY OPENINGS from outside trim edge to outside trim edge. (Make a note if the wood trim is wider than the standard 2 inches.)

CHECK COMBINED MEASUREMENTS of opposing walls to see whether they match. Many spaces are not

Basic plan view

Use the architectural symbols shown on page 65 and the example *below* to draw a bird's-eye view of your finished space. Be sure to include all the elements, from closets to new windows, skylights, outlets, and switches.

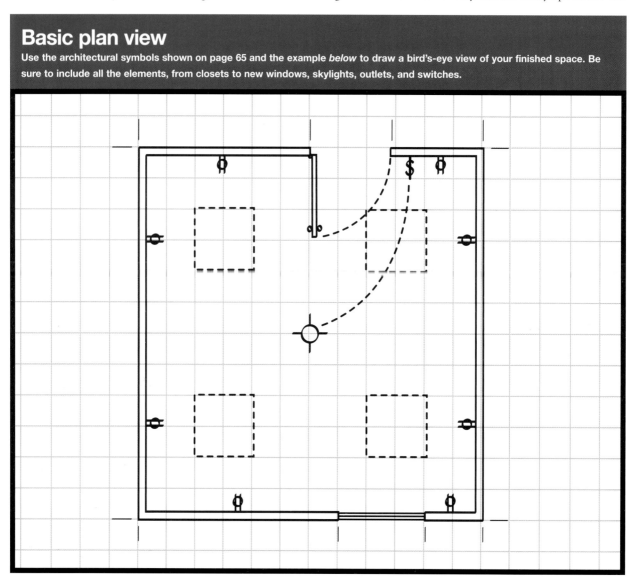

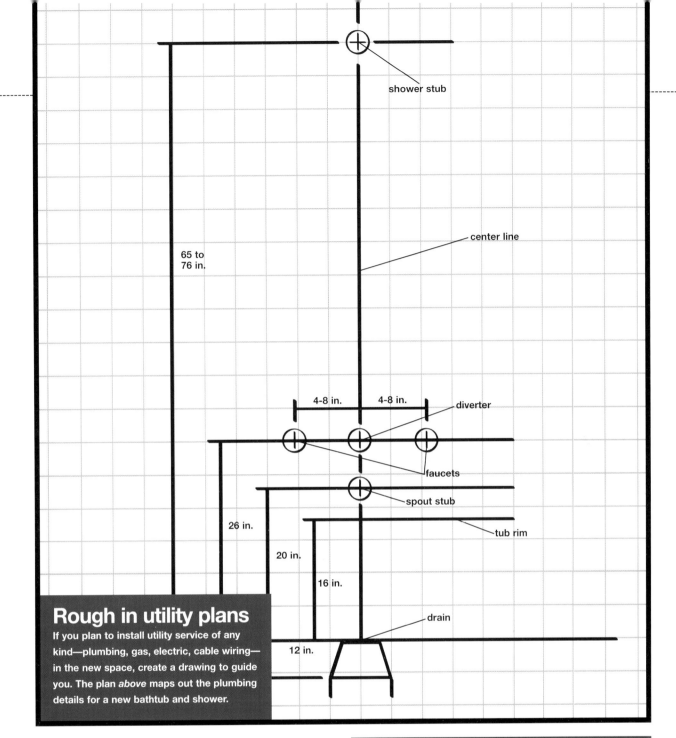

shower stub

center line

65 to 76 in.

4-8 in. 4-8 in.

diverter

faucets

spout stub

tub rim

26 in.

20 in.

16 in.

drain

12 in.

Rough in utility plans

If you plan to install utility service of any kind—plumbing, gas, electric, cable wiring—in the new space, create a drawing to guide you. The plan *above* maps out the plumbing details for a new bathtub and shower.

perfectly square but, if more than an inch difference exists, you may need to make some adjustments as you work.

RECORD VERTICAL PLACEMENT of fixed features, such as windows, fireplaces, and ceilings in a notebook or on an elevation drawing, one for each wall.

MEASURE TWICE. Really. Or have someone else do the measuring a second time then compare notes.

USE YOUR MEASUREMENTS to draw a final floor plan and wall elevation drawings if you'd like them. As with your rough plans, use a sharp pencil on graph paper with a scale of 1 square: 1 foot.

Go ahead, get an architect's professional help

You're quite capable of designing the revival of your basement as party central or your attic as a lofty retreat—but you'll save time and hassles by getting a pro's opinion as well. In addition, designing your space with the help of an architect often leads to nifty solutions—including budget-savvy ideas—that make your finished space even more successful. You can also tap an architect's expertise to review your own plans as insurance against any planning oversights. Consulting an architect especially makes sense as your plans grow in complexity.

dormers:
what shape roof?

Dormer strategies

Your house will look balanced when dormer windows align directly above windows or doors below them or are strategically lined up with spaces between windows beneath them.

gable dormers

shed dormers

If you're planning to add one or more dormers to your attic to increase the amount of headroom and living space, you need to choose from two basic structural styles. Gable dormers often are chosen for their traditional good looks, but shed dormers are easier to build and yield more usable space.

Dormers change the appearance of a home's exterior dramatically. If they are well-proportioned and harmonize with the existing architecture, they become a visual asset. Build your dormers large enough to be worth the trouble but not so large as to be overwhelming. Front walls of both gable and shed dormers either sit back from the main house wall or align with it. Align and style windows within dormers to match the existing windows beneath them.

Both sides now

A common strategy used to increase attic headroom *below* is to add gable dormers facing front and a shed dormer facing the back of the house.

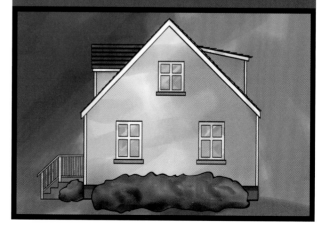

Dormer styles

Structurally speaking, all dormers are either gable or shed, but they can be finished in an endless array of forms. Choose a style that's consistent with the exterior features and architecture of your home.

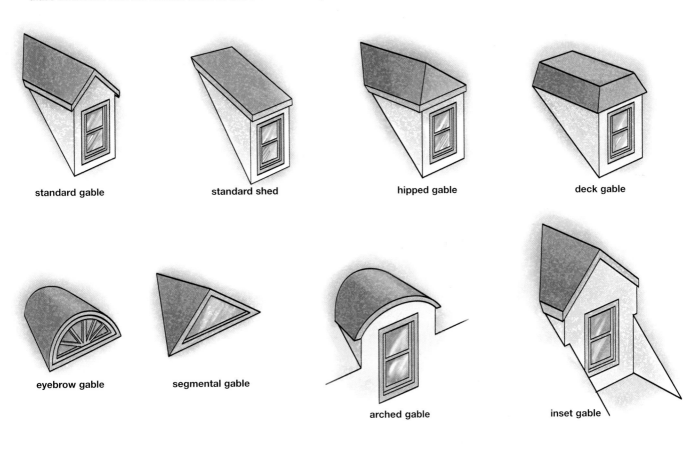

standard gable

standard shed

hipped gable

deck gable

eyebrow gable

segmental gable

arched gable

inset gable

To wall or not to wall

You can build a dormer with walls of any height or none at all. Dormers create intriguing architecture in the living spaces beneath them. Consider letting the ceiling beneath your dormer follow the roofline. Doing so adds to the drama and character of the space.

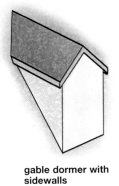

gable dormer with sidewalls

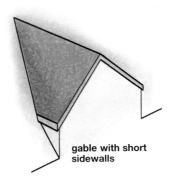

gable with short sidewalls

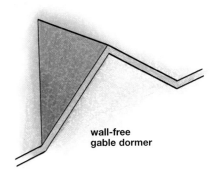

wall-free gable dormer

plan your storage

Living space needs storage space to support it, so don't commit every inch of your new project's floor space to new living area. The illustrations *right* show absolute minimum dimensions for conventional and walk-in closets. Build enough storage space to hold everything you need to store in the room you're creating, plus everything you currently store in the unfinished space. A full wall of shelving and cabinetry, attractively arranged around a media center or fireplace, is one high-capacity solution. Another is to reserve a small room for storage only.

Make an open-and-shut case for laundry

If your transformed basement displaces a sprawling, baskets-everywhere laundry room, resolve the issue with an organized laundry-in-a-closet like the one shown *below*. You need a 6×3-foot slice of space (perhaps a portion of a storage wall). Fit the closet with a 4-foot fluorescent lighting fixture and a shelf to hold detergent and other laundry necessities. You also need:

ACCESS TO UTILITIES hot and cold water supply lines, a drainage system, and electrical outlets.

AN EXTERIOR WALL LOCATION so that the dryer can be vented to the outdoors.

A FLOOR DRAIN to handle overflows or leaks. To achieve the required amount of drop-per-length positioning for your drainpipe, you may need to position the appliances on a platform. Consult a plumbing professional or your local building code official for assistance.

Alternatively, locate a stacking washer and dryer on one side of the closet, with shelves and hang-dry space on the other.

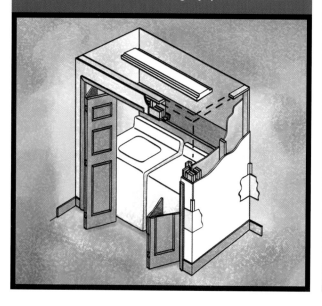

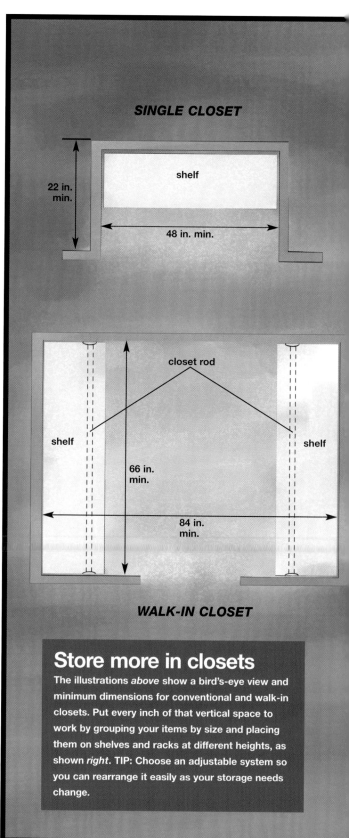

SINGLE CLOSET

shelf

22 in. min.

48 in. min.

closet rod

shelf   shelf

66 in. min.

84 in. min.

WALK-IN CLOSET

Store more in closets

The illustrations *above* show a bird's-eye view and minimum dimensions for conventional and walk-in closets. Put every inch of that vertical space to work by grouping your items by size and placing them on shelves and racks at different heights, as shown *right*. TIP: Choose an adjustable system so you can rearrange it easily as your storage needs change.

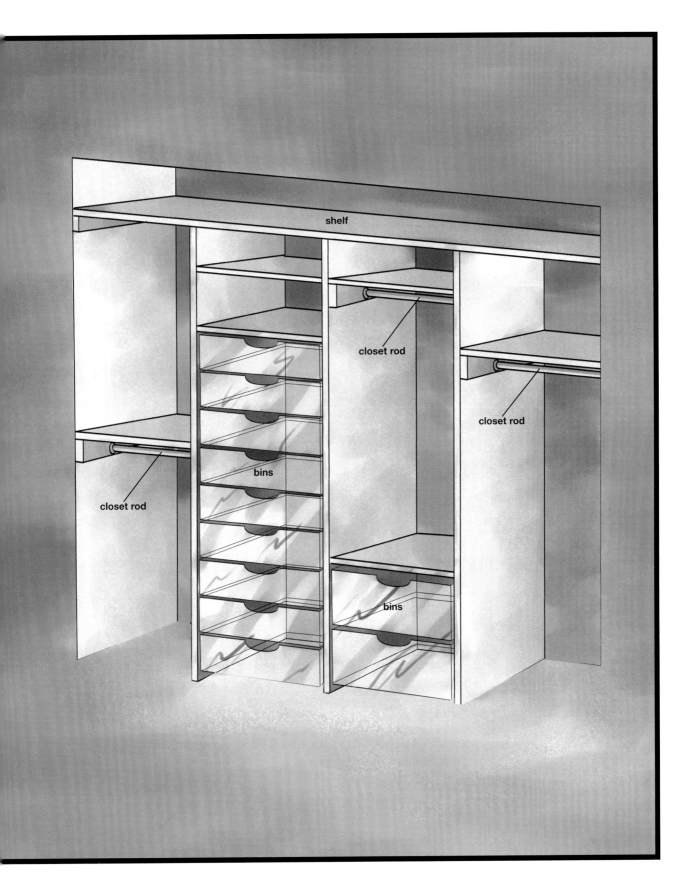

shelf

closet rod

closet rod

closet rod

closet rod

bins

bins

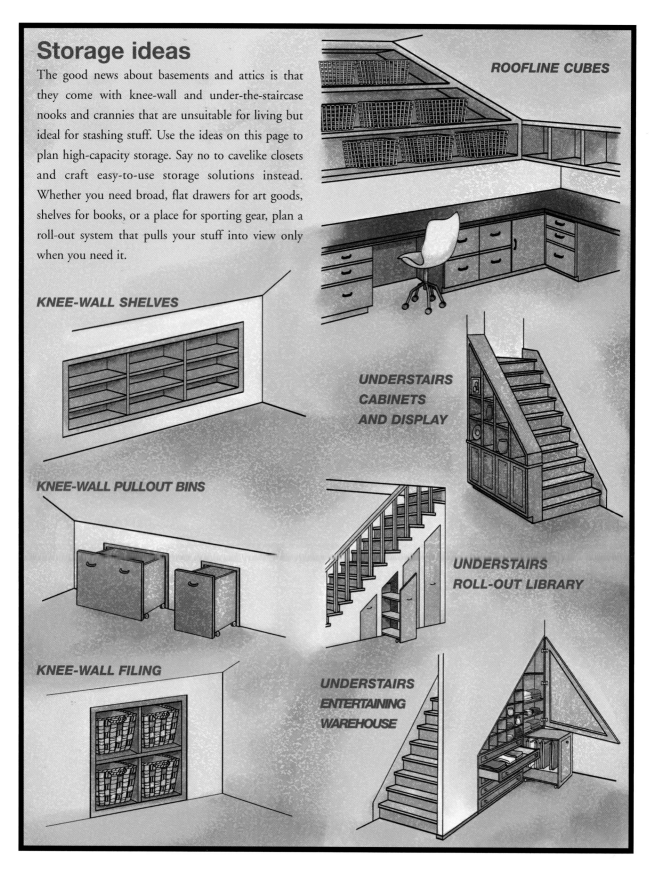

Storage ideas

The good news about basements and attics is that they come with knee-wall and under-the-staircase nooks and crannies that are unsuitable for living but ideal for stashing stuff. Use the ideas on this page to plan high-capacity storage. Say no to cavelike closets and craft easy-to-use storage solutions instead. Whether you need broad, flat drawers for art goods, shelves for books, or a place for sporting gear, plan a roll-out system that pulls your stuff into view only when you need it.

ROOFLINE CUBES

KNEE-WALL SHELVES

KNEE-WALL PULLOUT BINS

KNEE-WALL FILING

UNDERSTAIRS CABINETS AND DISPLAY

UNDERSTAIRS ROLL-OUT LIBRARY

UNDERSTAIRS ENTERTAINING WAREHOUSE

Simple saunas

Imagine slipping into your very own hot sauna after a tough day at work. You can! In Scandinavia it's common for families to enjoy their saunas every day. Such luxury—and all the healthy benefits that go with it—is a surprisingly simple project. So think about sliding one into your finished basement, attic, or bonus room. All you need is a 3×4-foot space, structural walls to frame the shell, and electric hookups. Prepackaged sauna kits include all the equipment, controls, and interior finish materials you need. Saunas use dry heat and require a 110-volt household current; there's no need for a separate circuit or plumbing and drains. Search the Internet for sauna kits; you'll find several companies that offer them in sizes ranging from 3×4 to 12×12 at prices that vary widely. The most affordable kits have walls that are lined with hemlock, spruce, and fir, and have fewer, more modest features in terms of light fixtures, backrests, towel bars, and timing controls. Pricier kits feature cedar or redwood walls and greater amenities. The relaxing effect of a sauna is the same no matter your choice. But, more importantly, installing a sauna is easy enough that it will relieve, not inspire, home improvement headaches.

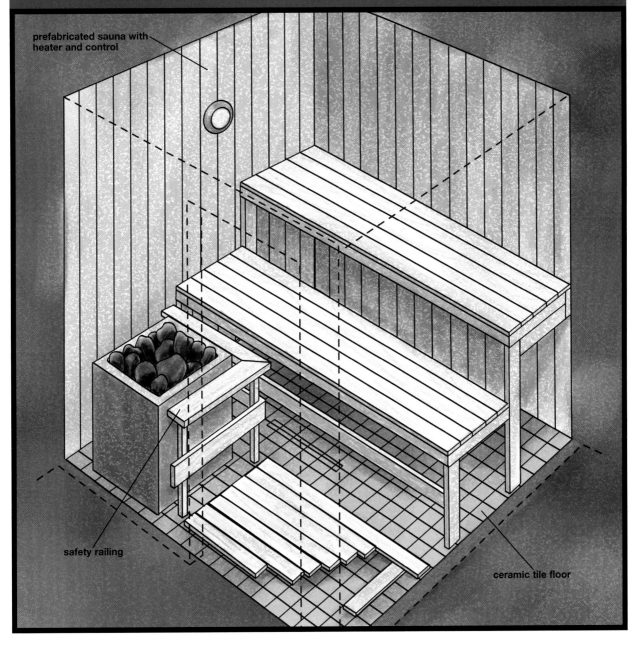

prefabricated sauna with heater and control

safety railing

ceramic tile floor

who will do the work?

You have four options for getting the work done. Each comes with both advantages and disadvantages.

DO ALL OR MOST OF THE WORK YOURSELF If you have the tools, skills, time, inclination, energy, and physical ability, you can save a lot of money by doing much of the work yourself. But before you tear into a big project, do a realistic self-assessment. Read the chapters that pertain to the jobs you're considering. Total up the cost of the additional tools, if any, you'll have to buy or rent to get the project done. Account for the time you'll likely spend on the work, along with the time it will take you to order and pick up materials and learn unfamiliar techniques. If you plan to take time off from your profession to complete the project, compute the cost of lost earnings. Then consider the cost of a potential mistake in both time and money. Miscutting a piece of wallboard may cost a few dollars in wasted material and a few minutes of time (if you've purchased an extra sheet or two for just such a situation). Miscutting a piece of sheet vinyl flooring or expensive carpet might cost hundreds. Wrestling with heavy materials or trying to work long hours to maintain a schedule sometimes results in injury, an even greater cost. It may actually be cheaper and less risky to hire out some jobs, such as laying carpet or sheet flooring, or extensive wiring or plumbing modifications, to specialists. Doing so allows you to concentrate on jobs that better suit your skills, tool collection, physical condition, and confidence level.

DO SOME OF THE WORK YOURSELF and hire out the rest. One way to do this is to position yourself as general contractor; another is to hire a general contractor. Either way, you pencil yourself in as the responsible party for certain tasks. Make sure you stick to schedule, though. Here's a handful of strategies for mixing up who does what:
MANAGE THE MATERIALS Order, purchase, and arrange delivery of supplies yourself.
BE A LABORER Do work that requires more labor than materials and skill: demolition, excavating, insulating, painting.
DO THE COSTLY WORK If you have the skills and tools, and if code allows, tackle the plumbing or electrical tasks, and leave less specialized efforts to others.
SWEAT THE SMALL STUFF. Ask your contractor to leave minor jobs—such as daily cleanup—and other tasks that require less than half a day—for you to do.

HIRE A GENERAL CONTRACTOR to complete the entire project. This is the most turnkey approach to getting your renovation completed. You hire one person with broad construction expertise to manage materials, inspections, and supervise the work of many others. That person is your primary contact.

Find a good, licensed contractor by asking friends and colleagues to recommend contractors who conducted successful jobs in their homes. It's a good idea to get several names and to meet with each. Doing so is time-consuming, but it's critical; the right contractor could become your partner for a succession of projects. When you meet with each contractor, discuss your plans, ask about his or her experience with similar projects, and how he or she would approach this one. Ask how much the project might cost—not as a formal, contractual estimate but to get a read on his or her familiarity with the work. Before the meeting ends ask for proof of bonding (to ensure your work will be completed), proof of insurance that covers on-the-job injuries and, most important, references. Talk to at least two customers who have had projects done that are similar to yours. Ask whether the work was done on time, on budget, and to their satisfaction. Arrange to view the work so you can assess the quality firsthand. Also ask to view a couple of projects that are currently under way, and talk to those homeowners too.

BE YOUR OWN GENERAL CONTRACTOR If your skills are more administrative than technical, filling the role of general contractor can be a great source of pride. As such you manage the purchase and delivery of materials, hire subcontractors, communicate plans to each, coordinate work schedules and inspections, and pay everyone. Select subcontractors carefully. Most subcontractors favor professional contractors over one-time do-it-yourself generals, because professionals are more likely to be a continual source of work.

Share the wealth

Transforming the walk-out basement entertaining area *above* required design, plumbing, electrical, general construction, drywall, carpentry, and flooring efforts. A homeowner can do all or some of the work as available skills, time, and tools allow.

Built-in decorative punch

If you have basic carpentry skills, knee-wall shelves are a simple project you can handle yourself. Tucked under a low-pitched attic roof, a chunk of knee-wall space *above* becomes a decorative display space. Cut into a marine blue and white-trimmed wall, the shelves' yellow-painted back adds punch and personality.

Getting bids on your project

The bidding process is the same whether you're getting a bid on a complete project from a general contractor or on a portion of the work from a subcontractor. Request bids based on your plans from a handful of the contractors you meet initially. If you have in mind specific appliances or features that you want to include in your project, list them and give the list to the bidding contractors. Three weeks is a reasonable amount of time for each of them to get back to you with a bid. When bids return, expect to find the following information: specific, itemized materials lists; a schedule noting what will be done when and when payments will be made based on that progress; and the contractor's fee. Remember that bid prices are not necessarily predictors of the quality of work or materials received, so ask contractors to explain their bids in detail.

Preparing your own estimate

If you'll be doing most of the work yourself, determine your costs by breaking the work into manageable chunks, starting with the costs for waterproofing and/or insulating, then framing, plumbing, electrical, and construction, then finish work. Rather than shopping at many different stores for the best prices on individual items, find one home center and lumber source that offers reasonable prices and top-notch service. Save yourself time and hassle by getting to know the sales staff at your chosen store. Make a habit of visiting when the store isn't busy and sharing your plans with the staff. A good salesperson can become an invaluable partner when you're estimating what each phase of your project will cost.

Be ready for the 10–15 rule

No matter how carefully you or your contractor(s) prepare bids, savvy homeowners know that a remodeling project generally ends up costing 10 to 15 percent more than estimated. Unexpected situations (see "Expect the unexpected" on page 98) and changes are commonplace. After hammers start swinging, enthusiastic homeowners often upgrade plans and materials, figuring "as long as we've gone to this much trouble, let's go further." Spare yourself hassle and headache by anticipating budget overruns.

Final contracts: signing on the dotted line

Bids are in; you've chosen your contractor(s). The next step is to protect everyone involved with a written contract that includes these features:

A DETAILED DESCRIPTION of work to be done by the contractor and subcontractors, as well as the work to be done by you. Include demolition and construction responsibilities.

A SCHEDULE OF WORK that also describes how delays will be handled and when payments will be made.

A COMPLETE DESCRIPTION of materials used.

PROTECTIVE ELEMENTS include a right-of-recision clause, which gives you a short period of time to back out of the project; proof of bonding and an insurance certifi-cate; a warranty that guarantees work and materials for at least one year; and a mechanic's lien waiver. (This protects you from having a lien placed against your property if your contractor doesn't pay the subcontractors.)

STATEMENTS THAT SPECIFY who secures building permits and arranges inspections.

A STATEMENT ABOUT CHANGE ORDERS and how modifications to planned work or last-minute "while-you're-here" additions to the work will be handled.

A STATEMENT THAT GUARANTEES FINAL WALK-THROUGH AND APPROVAL preceding final payment. During the meeting, point out anything that is not to your satisfaction. Allow the contractor a reasonable amount of time to remedy unsatisfactory situations.

Give me the money!

Remodeling plans and financing decisions will be intertwined if you plan to apply for a home improvement loan. Many loan sources require you to produce a full set of plans and bids. Some loan sources require that all or part of the project be completed by a professional; it's not unusual for a loan representative to inspect the work and make payments directly to contractors.

CASH IS THE SIMPLEST WAY to pay for your basement, attic, or bonus room transformation. Write a check or use your credit card and pay off the monthly charges.

A HOME EQUITY LINE of credit, essentially a loan written against the equity of your home, has a lot of appeal. These credit lines allow you to write checks against the line and repay the money in regular payments or in large amounts as you have it. Interest is usually tax-deductible.

A HOME IMPROVEMENT LOAN, second mortgage, or refinancing of your first mortgage for a larger amount is more cumbersome to arrange and requires that you forecast the final cost of your project. Some homeowners arrange a home equity line of credit to fund the project while it's under way, then pay off the line with a second mortgage or by refinancing their first mortgage when the project is completely finished.

LOW-COST, AND SOMETIMES FORGIVABLE, IMPROVEMENT LOANS are available in many cities for developing or historic neighborhoods or for people in low-income situations. Your local building code official, city planner, or historic society may be able to direct you to programs that help cut the cost of financing your remodeling work.

Surviving the remodeling process

The good news is that basements, attics, and bonus rooms rate low on the remodeling stress scale. Their out-of-the-way locations mean that you can close the door on the mess at the end of the day. That's something you can't do when you're remodeling your kitchen!

Still you can make the process go more smoothly for you and your family if you do some advance planning.

WATERPROOF YOUR BASEMENT then live with it through at least one heavy rain season to make sure it stays dry before you remodel the space.

REMOVE ACTIVITY AREAS from the affected spaces during remodeling. It's tough to do laundry when the basement is full of sawdust.

CLOSE OFF ENTRIES If your family usually goes in and out of the house through the space you're remodeling, train them to use other entries before work begins.

Create hassle-free living with universal design

You may be familiar with Universal Design as a set of architectural concepts that make a home more livable for the handicapped or elderly. In actuality, Universal Design is about flexibility and easy access. Incorporating Universal Design aspects into your basement, attic, or bonus room project creates a more comfortable space and makes using the space easier for anyone suffering a bad back, using crutches or a wheelchair temporarily, or healing from a broken arm or leg. A handful of Universal Design concepts follows. For more information on carrying the concept further, search your library or the Internet for Universal or Accessible Home Design.

UTILIZE THE COMFORTABLE REACH RANGE Put door handles, appliances, electrical switches, and outlets 15 to 48 inches above the floor, and everyone will be able to reach them comfortably.

FIT CUPBOARDS AND CABINETS WITH ROLL-OUT drawers, so contents can be pulled into view.

CHOOSE REFRIGERATOR DRAWERS over traditional stand-up models.

CRAFT THRESHOLD-FREE, STEP-FREE ENTRIES and plan bump-free transitions between flooring materials.

MAKE SINK COUNTERS no taller than 34 inches; allow knee clearance of 27 inches high, 30 inches wide, and 19 inches deep. Choose lever or wrist-blade-style faucets and scald-proof, thermostatically controlled valves.

IN BATHS arrange curb-free shower rooms with handheld, height-adjustable showerheads. Frame the walls with blocking, so you can install grab bars when needed.

ALLOW 4-FOOT PASSAGEWAYS from one space to the next.

ALLOW 5-FOOT approach room near beds and activity areas. This allows wheelchairs room to turn around.

A desk for everyone

A cantilevered length of laminate countertop lines two adjacent walls in this colorful basement and provides a flexible desk situation for everyone in the family. The leg-free surface remains clear of obstacles, making it an easy surface for someone to roll up to. A freestanding stack of drawers can be slid underneath the desk to boost storage capacity.

IDENTIFY THE PATH you want contractors (or anyone else) to use to get through the house. Protect the floors along this path by taping plastic sheeting over them.

SEAL OFF THE WORK AREA by hanging several sheets of plastic, floor to ceiling, around doors that separate the work area from the rest of your home.

SWEEP AND CLEAN UP DAILY Dust, grime, and scraps that travel into the house on your shoes are tough on floors and carpet.

SCHEDULE A TIME each day to discuss project progress and situations. This may well be the most important tip, whether you're doing the work yourself or hiring it out. Some families find that reviewing the day's work when they arrive home tired and hungry is stressful and leads to rash judgments. A better choice is to hold off any review until everyone has had dinner and a chance to relax.

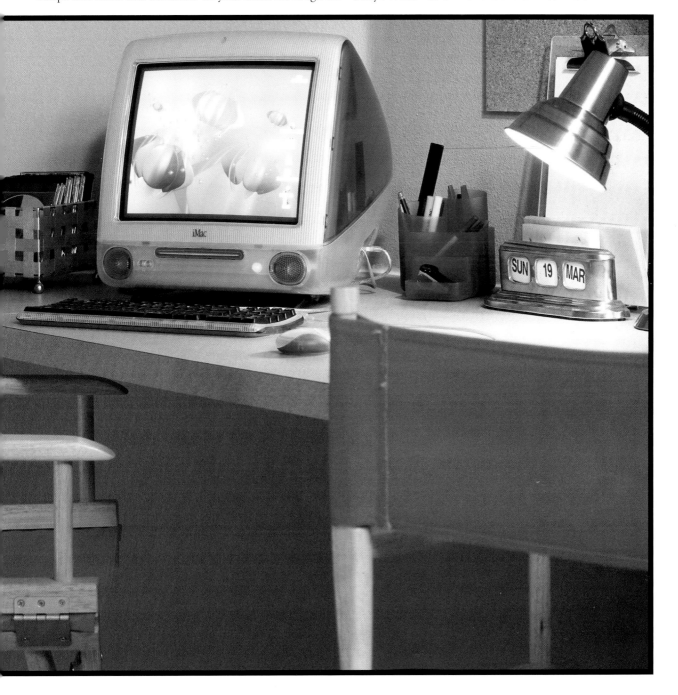

A pair of trios

Two shed dormers *above*, each three windows wide, lift the roof of this third-floor attic and nearly double the available floor space. Dormers were the best option in this case, where a full third level would have made the house appear massive.

As you begin a remodeling project, be ready to meet the unexpected along the way. And just to be safe, plan on tapping your sense of humor and flexibility too. Whether you'll be working underground or in the trees, here's a short list of what you may discover.

Water damage

Brownish stains, visible in basements on the first-floor subflooring, and in attics on insulation sheathing, indicate a previous or present water leak. If the stain is spongy, the leak is active. Find the source of the leak and repair it; then repair or replace affected materials. If you have trouble finding the source of the leak, you can purchase a professional leak detection test, which costs about two hundred dollars. Attic leaks usually start at the rooftop and need to be repaired up there. Check for leaks using a hose and running water. Direct water around flashing and materials around vents, chimneys, and any other openings, to find the leak source. Some leaks make themselves evident on the interior away from where the water actually enters, so to be sure you find the source. Start at the lowest point of the roof and slowly work your way upward. Have a helper look for the presence of water inside while you wet down the outside.

Insect trouble

Check framing and joists for sawdust, pinholes, and soft spots that give way to a screwdriver. All these point to insect infestations. Hire an exterminator to treat the problem. You may also need to repair or replace the affected area.

Mold

Water damage and high humidity cause mold to grow within walls. If you find mold remove it and locate the source of excess water (see page 140). Often you can remove mold simply by applying a 50 percent solution of laundry bleach and water to the affected area (be sure to provide plenty of ventilation). If mold growth is extensive, you may have to replace carpet, insulation, and other affected materials.

Asbestos

Asbestos often lurks underneath siding or inside the ductwork in the basements of homes and in resilient flooring materials, insulation that surrounds furnaces or wood-burning stoves, and roofing. Asbestos in good condition usually releases no dangerous particles and is best left alone. However, if the material has tears, abrasions, or water damage, you may be exposed to its fibers which, when inhaled, can cause lung cancer and other health problems. If you have damaged material that you suspect contains asbestos, hire a professional to test it. Don't do the test yourself; you can inadvertently release more fibers. If the material contains asbestos, it must be professionally sealed, covered, or removed. Removal is not always the best option due to the risk of releasing more fibers. Contact your local Environmental Protection Agency office to find a licensed asbestos testing and removal agent.

Lead-based paint

The federal government banned lead-based paint in 1978, but most homes built before then still contain it. Lead poses health threats to children and pregnant women. Lead-based paint that's in good condition is rarely hazardous. It becomes a problem only when it's peeling, chipping, or cracking and can be ingested. Have your home professionally tested before beginning a remodeling project. A test identifies the lead content of painted surfaces and determines whether there are serious sources of lead exposure. If a lead hazard exists, professionals can remove, seal, or enclose it. Find a state-certified lead professional by calling 888/532-3547.

Radon

Odorless, colorless radon is a natural gas often present in basements. Because it has been linked to lung cancer, radon at a high level is a health threat. Test your home with a do-it-yourself kit purchased at a home center or hire a professional. If high levels exist seek advice from a radon abatement technician. (See "Radon Testing" in your directory.) Solutions involve sealing cracks and joints, and using fans and ducts to circulate fresh air.

6

tools

TOOLS ARE THE MEANS TO THE END: The right ones help you get the job done quickly, safely, and well. Carefully chosen, high-quality tools are a good investment—not only in your current project but in future ones as well. Good tools pay for themselves again and again, both in the money saved by not having to hire professionals to do the work for you and in the freedom and pride that come from knowing you have the means to improve your living space to suit your lifestyle.

Start your tool collection by purchasing only what you need for the job at hand; then gradually add to your collection as the scope of your work expands. You probably don't need the top-of-the-line, most expensive models, but good-quality tools will last through many years of service, so buy the best you can afford.

This chapter walks you through the different power and hand tools you may need for both demolition and construction. It talks about safety equipment, tool accessories, and tools you can rent for specialized jobs. You'll also learn about multifunction tools—versatile items that pack many functions into a single unit that's easy to use and store. Finally you'll find some suggestions on how to organize, transport, and store your tools so you always have what you need nearby.

OPPOSITE: Good-quality tools make your job easier and more pleasurable and, in the case of fine hand tools, they may well serve your needs for a lifetime. Fortunately most of the tools you need for remodeling a basement, attic, or bonus room can be put to use on just about any other remodeling project you can imagine. The few specialty tools you may need can be rented inexpensively.

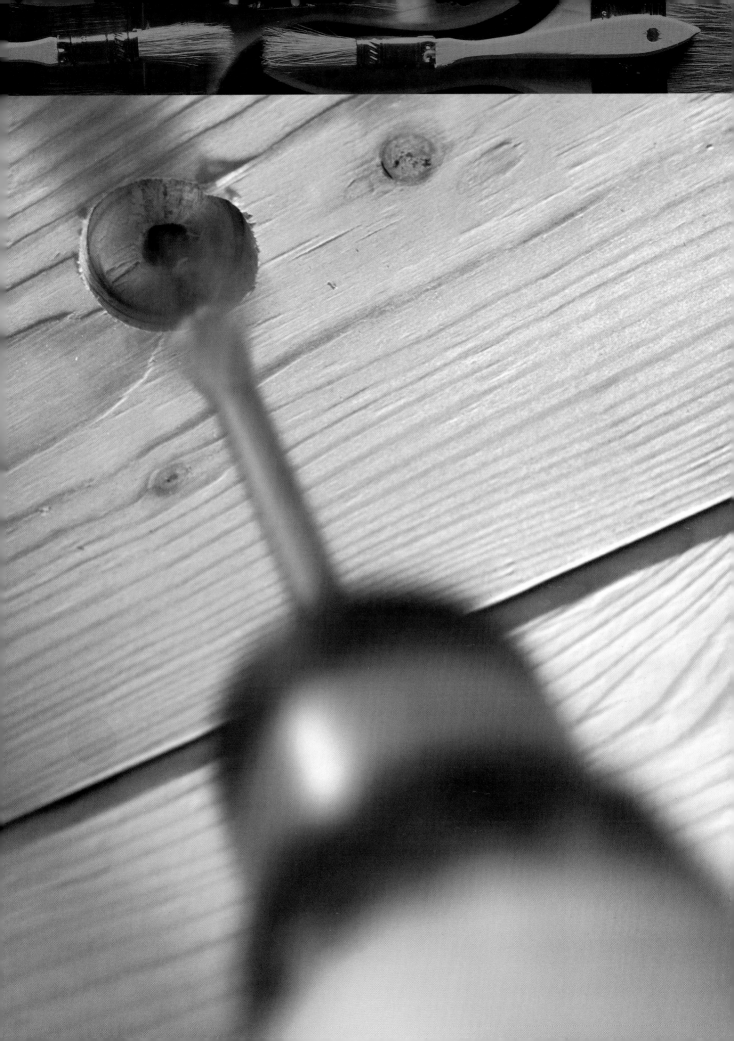

Measurement and layout tools

These tools help you plan, lay out, and build a project.

1. TAPE MEASURES provide a compact ruler for all measuring tasks. Thirteen-foot models are most common and slip easily into a pocket; 26-footers are bulkier but handle just about any interior measurement you need.

2. COMBINATION SQUARES let you draw square lines across boards for cutting. They are also handy for marking layouts a specific distance in from the edge of a board.

3. LAYOUT SQUARES (also called speed squares) do many of the same tasks as combination squares. They also serve as circular saw guides, helping you to make perfectly square crosscuts. Some models can cut at various angles, which makes cutting roof rafters, for example, easy.

4. FRAMING SQUARES help make sure larger layouts, such as those for tile floors and stud walls, are square.

5. T-BEVELS transfer angles from one place to another.

6. LEVELS come in many lengths. Start with a line level and a small torpedo level. You'll also want a 3- or 4-foot carpenter's level for accurate, large-scale work.

7. PLUMB BOBS, heavy, pointed weights dangling from a string, provide a vertical reference.

8. CHALK LINES are used to draw long, straight lines. Get one that reels into a weighted metal case that serves as a plumb bob and can be filled with powdered chalk. The string rechalks every time you rewind it and will be ready to snap a line every time it's extended.

9. STUD FINDERS help locate framing studs behind walls. Electronic and magnetic finders detect the nails in a wall but can be fooled by wires and pipes. New models use sound to sense the density of the studs.

Demolition tools

1. 3-LB. HAMMERS are useful for demolishing almost anything that can be removed in several pieces.

2. RIPPING BARS use the lever principle to multiply your muscle power, helping you take just about anything apart, from a cabinet to a whole wall. Usually this entails destroying whatever it is you're removing.

3. CAT'S PAWS remove big nails, such as those that hold wall studding together.

4. FLAT PRY BARS are great for general prying, such as removing cabinet frames from floors and walls.

5. PUTTY KNIVES pry off moldings without damage.

6. COLD CHISELS score and cut masonry.

Construction tools

1. 16-OUNCE CLAW HAMMERS are heavy enough

to drive large nails, yet small enough for use when installing moldings.

2. 21-OUNCE FRAMING HAMMERS drive big nails.

3. 12-OUNCE TACK HAMMERS install trim.

4. NAIL SETS drive nails below the surface of moldings and extend your reach into hard-to-hammer places.

5. SCREWDRIVERS, both straight blade and phillips blade, are necessary for installing hardware.

6. AWLS are pointed tools used for marking hole locations and starting screws.

7. UTILITY KNIVES do everything from sharpening your pencil to cutting insulation and drywall. Keep plenty of blades on hand and replace them often.

8. COPING SAWS are indispensable for cutting moldings at inside corners.

9. MITER BOXES AND BACKSAWS make accurate crosscuts and miters in molding. Choose a motorized version (called a power miter saw or a chop saw) if you are making a lot of angled cuts, for example, when installing molding.

10. CHISELS pare and fine-tune the fit of door hinges and other hardware. Purchase a set that includes ¼-inch, ½-inch, ¾-inch, and 1-inch blade widths.

11. PLANES make short work of trimming a door to size and smoothing, straightening, and squaring wood.

12. HEAVY-DUTY METAL SNIPS are useful for a variety of metal-cutting tasks.

13. ONE-HANDED CLAMPS are handy for a variety of jobs, such clamping cabinets together before fastening them.

14. SPRING CLAMPS are for light-duty clamping.

Drywall tools

Installing drywall—laying out, cutting, taping, applying compound over the fasteners and sheet joints, and smoothing the dried compound—requires a special set of tools.

1. DRYWALL SQUARES lay out and guide cuts on a sheet of drywall.

2. UTILITY KNIVES are great for cutting drywall, as well as rigid-foam or fiberglass bat insulation.

3. JAB SAWS make interior cutouts, such as those around electrical boxes.

4. DRYWALL KNIVES are used for spreading joint compound and come in various widths. Most jobs can be handled with three—a 6-inch, 10-inch, and 12-inch blade.

5. MUD PANS allow you to carry joint compound (or mud) as you work. A mud pan is shaped to accommodate wider drywall knives and has a tough metal edge along its rim for scraping excess compound from tools.

6. DRYWALL SANDERS have a replaceable sanding screen and a holder to mount it on. The holder has a dust pickup that attaches to the hose of a shop vacuum to minimize dust.

7. CORDLESS DRILL-DRIVER drives drywall screws.

8. INSIDE CORNER TAPING TOOL smooths tape on inside corners.

9. CORNER CRIMPING TOOL crimps corner bead on outside corners.

10. SHEET LIFTER lifts drywall sheets into place.

Painting tools

1. ROLLER TRAY AND LINER hold paint.

2. TRIM ROLLER paints small surfaces.

3. DROP CLOTH AND MASKING TAPE keep paint off floors, furniture, and adjoining surfaces.

4. ROLLER AND ROLLER COVER applies paint quickly to large surfaces.

5. PAINT GUARD moves along with your brush to keep paint off adjoining surfaces.

6. BRUSHCOMB straightens paintbrush bristles and aids in cleaning brushes.

7. PAINTBRUSH AND ANGLED SASH BRUSH are used for trim, cutting in, and window sashes.

8. EDGER creates a neat, sharp line where two surfaces meet, such as where a wall meets a ceiling.

9. ROLLER HANDLE EXTENSIONS extend your reach when painting tall walls or ceilings.

Flooring tools

1. FLAT PRY BAR AND PUTTY KNIFE help pry loose shoe moldings with minimal damage.

2. **CHALK LINE** makes marking layout lines a snap.

3. **SMOOTH AND NOTCHED TROWELS** apply and spread grout and adhesive.

4. **COMBINATION AND FRAMING SQUARES** ensure materials are cut square and lines are perpendicular.

5. **FILE** trims nails flush with molding for reinstallation.

6. **FLOORING KNIFE** cuts linoleum and resilient tile.

7. **KNEE PADS** make kneeling during installation more comfortable.

Plumbing tools

1. **PIPE WRENCH** grips and loosens threaded pipe.

2. **PLIERS** grip and hold fittings.

3. **CARPENTER'S LEVEL** checks pipe for correct slope.

4. **PROPANE TORCH** solders copper pipe.

5. **BASIN WRENCH** grips nuts you can't reach with pliers.

6. **FLARING TOOL** makes flare joints in copper tubing.

7. **TUBING CUTTER** cuts copper pipe and tubing.

8. **CAULKING GUN** seals joints around fixtures.

9. **GROOVE-JOINT PLIERS** grip pipes and fittings.

10. **PLASTIC-TUBING CUTTER** cuts plastic supply pipe.

11. **ADJUSTABLE-END WRENCH** fits the nuts on faucets and other fixtures.

Wiring tools

1. RECEPTACLE ANALYZER tells if a receptacle has a bad connection and if it is properly grounded and polarized.

2. SOLDERING GUN AND SOLDER solders wire.

3. DIGITAL VOLTMETER indicates voltage at an outlet.

4. CONTINUITY TESTER tests fuses, switches, and sockets.

5. WIRE NUTS fasten wires together.

6. SCREWDRIVERS remove mounting screws on switches and outlets, and tighten and loosen terminal screws.

7. ELECTRICAL TAPE insulates splices in wire.

Installation tools

1. COMBINATION TOOL strips, crimps, and cuts wire.

2. TONGUE-AND-GROOVE PLIERS tighten connectors.

3. HACKSAW cuts conduit and metal-sheathed cable.

4. SLIP-JOINT PLIERS tighten connectors.

5. KEYHOLE SAW cuts drywall.

6. BIT EXTENSION allows the drilling of deep holes in framing to run wire.

7. ADJUSTABLE WIRE STRIPPER strips wire.

8. LINEMAN'S PLIERS twist wires together and cut wire.

9. FISH TAPE pulls wire through wall cavities.

10. TAPE MEASURE measures wire runs and plots switch and outlet locations.

11. STUD SENSOR indicates the location of studs behind drywall.

12. BX CUTTER cuts metal-sheathed cable.

13. MINI-HACKSAW reaches where full-size hacksaws can't.

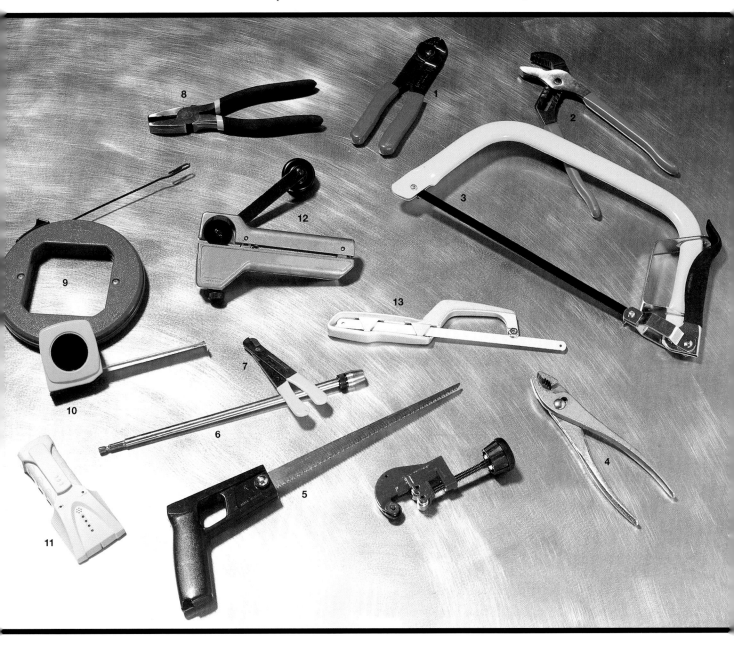

inside corners. Some models feature variable speed control, which is handy if you cut materials other than wood, such as plastic or metal. Orbital cutting saber saws cut faster than those without this feature.

3. RECIPROCATING SAWS are handy for demolition work. A variety of blades with teeth designed to cut different materials, including wood, nails, screws, and even steel pipe, are available. Blades can reach into tight places, such as between framing members.

4. POWER MITER SAWS, also called chop saws, are stationary circular saws. They make quick, clean crosscuts, but their forte is making extremely accurate mitered, or angled, cuts. If you have a lot of trim pieces to cut and install, a chop saw is the tool to use.

Drilling and shaping tools

A drill and some bits are all you need for most jobs. Add a router, and you can make your own moldings.

1. ⅜-INCH VARIABLE-SPEED REVERSIBLE (VSR) DRILLS handle almost all drilling needs. If you're going to drill a lot of holes in concrete, consider getting a hammer drill, which is capable of adding impact action similar to a jackhammer to help speed drilling into masonry. Otherwise a good, upper-mid-grade corded drill is adequate. Cheap homeowner models and cordless models don't have the power or torque necessary to handle drilling repeated

Saws

Four types of power saws accomplish almost every cut you'll need to make when renovating an attic or basement, from cutting openings in the roof for a dormer or skylight to installing molding.

1. 7¼-INCH CIRCULAR SAWS crosscut and rip lumber and plywood to the right size, making straight cuts with ease. If you buy only one power saw, this is the one to get. Steel blades dull quickly, so purchase more durable carbide-tipped combination blades.

2. SABER SAWS crosscut and rip, although much more slowly and with less smoothness and accuracy than circular saws. Their main function is cutting curves, but they also are indispensable for making small cutouts of any shape, as their thin blades start a cut almost anywhere you can drill a small hole. A saber saw is used instead of a handsaw to square off the crescent-shape cuts left by a circular saw when finishing

holes with hole saws and large spade bits. (For more information, see "Cordless power tools" *below*.)

2. TWIST DRILL BITS bore such things as pilot holes for screws. Buy a graduated set that's made of high-speed steel for durability.

3. SPADE BITS bore larger holes, such as those needed to install wiring inside a stud wall. Again buy a set of these to make sure you have the sizes you need on hand.

4. HOLE SAWS are powered by a drill to make large holes, such as those for a lockset in a door.

5. ROUTERS are useful for cutting decorative moldings and making mortises for door hinges.

Cordless power tools

Cordless tools have revolutionized the market. The most popular by far is the cordless drill/driver, but you can also find cordless reciprocating saws, circular saws, jigsaws, and miter saws.

Cordless tools offer increased portability and convenience and are especially valuable to professionals who constantly use their tools on the go. However, these tools have some disadvantages as well:

• **THEY USUALLY COST** more than corded versions.

• **USE AND RUN TIME** depends on the battery charge and capacity. The tool must be kept charged to be ready for use. (If you buy a cordless tool, keep two batteries. Use one battery while the other is recharging.)

• **BATTERIES** may be expensive to replace.

• **CORDLESS-TOOL BATTERIES** range from 7.2 to 24 volts. Drills come in all voltages; other tools, such as reciprocating saws, circular saws, jigsaws, and miter saws, come with high-voltage battery packs.

• **SOME CORDLESS TOOLS** simply aren't powerful enough for some jobs, such as drilling into concrete or making repeated bores with large spade bits.

• **CORDLESS DRILLS** are often heavier and larger than their corded counterparts, making them somewhat more fatiguing to hold and difficult to use in tight spots.

Cordless tools generally are sold with a charger designed to recharge their batteries. You'll find nickel-cadmium (NiCAD) batteries in most tools you shop for; those with

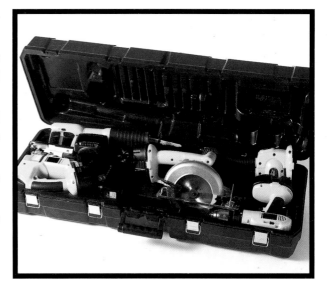

nickel metal hydride (NiMH) batteries usually are worth the extra cost. They provide more run time and faster recharging with less weight. If you own more than one drill/driver, the second tool should definitely be cordless, ideally 12 volts or more, with a ⅜-inch chuck, a two-speed transmission, and an adjustable clutch that kicks the motor out of gear when it reaches a preset torque level. (The last feature keeps you from breaking off screws or burying them in the wood as you drive them.)

Other cordless tools may be convenient, but you probably won't need their convenience enough to justify the added cost, weight, lower power output, and other drawbacks. The corded variety will probably serve your needs better.

Buy quality

Many of today's medium-priced tools boast features, power, and durability that once could be found only in pricey professional-grade tools. Cheaper tools suffice if you aren't concerned with long-term durability or accuracy. The best rule to follow for tool purchases is this: Buy only the tools you *really* need—but buy the highest-quality tools you can afford. When comparing tools use amperage ratings to compare power, rather than horsepower ratings, which can be deceiving. In general the more durable and long-lasting tools feature ball or needle bearings instead of bushings, precisely machined gears instead of die-cast or nonmetallic gears, one-piece housings, switches with dust boots, and hatches that enable you to change worn-out brushes.

Safety equipment

Buy these pieces of safety equipment when you buy the corresponding tools that require their use.

1. SAFETY GLASSES OR GOGGLES protect your eyes with industrial-quality safety glass. Buy a pair that has side shields and a "Z87.1" label, which tells you they're industrial strength. If you wear prescription glasses, either buy prescription safety glasses or get goggles that fit over them. If possible, try on glasses or goggles before you buy them. Find a pair so comfortable that you won't mind wearing them whenever you're working.

2. EARPLUGS OR EARMUFFS offer hearing protection from noisy power tools. Both types work well. Choosing from the two is largely a matter of personal preference. Try them on before you buy to find the most comfortable pair. If they are not comfortable, you are less likely to wear them.

3. DUST MASKS protect your lungs during demolition and drywall finishing. Check the label before you buy and match the mask you buy to the type of work you're doing. In general masks with a single strap are rated for nuisance dust. These masks work well to keep sawdust out of your lungs. But for sanding drywall or for ripping out plaster, you need a mask that's rated for fine dust. These thicker masks usually have two straps.

4. WORK GLOVES help you handle dirty work, such as unloading materials, demolition, and cleaning up debris. Do not wear them when you are working with power tools—you are more likely to lose your grip or fumble a tool or piece while wearing gloves. Gloves also can get caught in a spinning blade or drill bit. Rubber gloves protect your skin and prevent your hands from becoming dry and irritated when you apply joint compound or mix paint.

5. BOOTS are a good footwear choice when you're using power tools; cowhide boots offer more protection against cuts and bruises than lighter footgear. At the very least wear sturdy, rubber-soled shoes to prevent slipping.

6. FIRST AID KITS ensure that you're prepared with supplies in case of an accident or minor injury while you are working on your project.

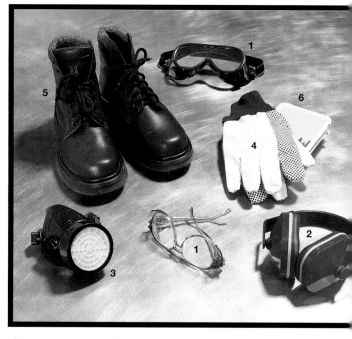

Accessories

Several items make working with hand and power tools a great deal easier.

1. EXTENSION CORDS made of heavy-duty, 12-gauge wire are preferable to lightweight cords, which can overheat, posing a fire or shock hazard and robbing the tools of the power they need. Always use three-pronged cords and grounded receptacles. When working outdoors plug the cord into a ground fault circuit interrupter (GFCI). Uncoil the cord so it doesn't develop kinks, which can damage the conductors. Protect the cord from sharp edges and, if it crosses a walkway, tape it down with duct tape.

2. SAWHORSES hold lumber at a comfortable working height. You can create an impromptu worktable by nailing a sheet of plywood between two horses. Wooden horses are heavier than metal models and offer two advantages: You can nail a couple of 2×4s across them for added stability, and you won't damage your saw blade if you cut into them.

3. WORK LIGHTS make working in a dimly lit place (exactly where most remodeling projects take place) simpler and more safe. Halogen models throw a brighter, whiter light than incandescent lights and often come with adjustable stands. Be careful, though; they get very hot.

Rental tools

Several tools are best rented due to their expense and the few times you will use them. Check with your local tool-rental shop to see what tools are available for rent.

DRYWALL HOISTS make hanging drywall a safer, less-strenuous, less-awkward task. If you have enough space to make use of one, renting a hoist is well worth the money.

DRYWALL SPRAYERS use an air compressor and a special gun to make quick, simple work of creating the rough "popcorn" finish often found on ceilings. If you have a small area to cover, buy an inexpensive hand-pump model.

LASER LEVELS are great for setting the initial layout line around the perimeter of a room when you are installing a drop ceiling.

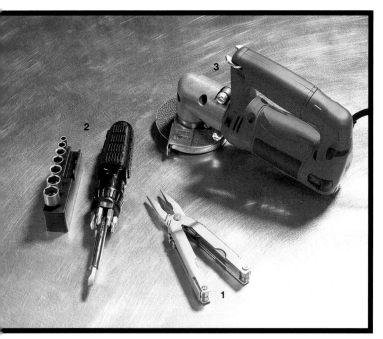

Multifunction tools

Some multifunction tools are a poor compromise, an attempt to do too much with too little. Others, however, are so versatile and well-designed you may wonder how you ever got along without them. Here are a few favorites, mentioned in the order of increasing size:

1. MULTITOOLS combine more than a dozen functions in one neat little folding unit in a tidy case that hangs from your belt. Typically they include pliers, wire cutters, screwdrivers, a file, a hacksaw blade, and the like. For production work they're no substitute for the real thing, but if you wear one whenever you're working on a project, you'll be amazed by how often you use it and how much time it saves compared to running back to your toolbox for every need. Get the best multitool you can find—cheapies are flimsy and useless.

2. RATCHETING SCREWDRIVERS AND BITS allow you to do most of the driving tasks you'll encounter—without having to carry a quiver full of straight-shanked drivers. Again purchase a good one, preferably with a handle that's hinged in the middle, so you can really bear down and twist when you need to. Get a complete set of bits for it—not just slotted and phillips heads in a variety of sizes, but also torx, square-drive, allen-head, and nut-driving sockets—you'll be able to take apart or put together almost anything.

3. SPIRAL SAWS save you lots of time if you're planning to remodel several rooms in your home. They're particularly handy for making quick cutouts in drywall, such as for switches and outlets, but they also cut wood, tile, cement board, and just about anything else. Get a model with an angle-grinding attachment so you can also make straight cuts in metal and other materials more quickly than with a hacksaw. You can use spiral saws to grind and polish too.

4. PORTABLE WORKBENCHES, sometimes called clamping benches, can be plunked down anywhere you need a work surface. The top is split in two, and a pair of cranks moves the two top pieces back and forth to hold material you're working on. Pegs slip into holes in the tabletop, allowing you to grab wide or irregularly shaped pieces. The table also can be used to hold tools firmly, such as a miter box, while in use.

5. COMBINATION LADDERS are contortionists that perform the functions of a whole collection of ladders and then some. They consist of four 4-foot-long ladder sections that are jointed together to fold up like an accordion into a neat rectangular package that's easy to transport. On the

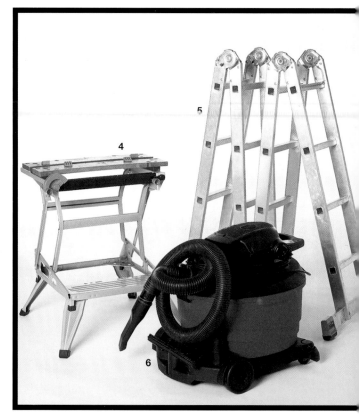

work site you can use it as a 4-, 8-, 12-, or 16-foot straight ladder (depending on how many sections you unfold); a 4- or 8-foot double stepladder; or an 8-foot-long, 4-foot-high work scaffold. You can also use it in an L shape as a stair or roof scaffold. Get one that has joint latches that are easy to use and click positively in place, and a commercial-duty, 300-lb. rating. Even if you weigh half that or less, you'll appreciate the rigidity of a high-capacity ladder. If you use it as a scaffold, resist the temptation to make your own scaffolding boards. Instead, buy those that are available as options from the manufacturer; they're more safe and secure than homemade versions.

6. SHOP VACUUMS are an essential antidote to the inevitably messy process of remodeling. Choose the combination wet-or-dry type, which quickly sucks up standing water and spills. Many vacuums have a detachable power head that allows you to convert the tool to a portable blower—great for cleaning large areas. For serious work get the 2-inch diameter suction hoses—the smaller, 1¼-inch hoses clog frequently. Smaller hoses work well when you're using the device as a portable dust-collection system; these hoses connect to the sawdust discharge ports on many tools. Unless you actually have a woodshop with stationary tools such as wood lathes that create huge volumes of chips and shavings, you don't need a huge machine. Easy portability is more important than huge capacity in this case.

Toting tools

A great tool collection is useless if it's not where you need it. Here's how to keep your tools organized and handy.

1. TOOL POUCHES are perhaps the best time- and frustration-saving tool you can buy. Without one you are constantly interrupting your work as you fetch tools you forgot to have on hand. Get in the habit of wearing your pouch and storing the same tools in the same pockets all the time. When you do you'll find that you reach for the right tool without thinking about it, freeing your mind to concentrate on the job at hand.

2. TOOL BAGS are a great way to organize and transport the tools you use most frequently. They look like old-fashioned doctor's bags, with loop handles and wide-opening gate mouths, except they're made of heavy canvas or cordura nylon instead of black leather. A multitude of pockets inside and out keeps tools organized and handy, and a huge main compartment is big enough to hold a power tool or two as well as the usual assortment of hammers, chisels, pry bars, and wrenches. Like soft-sided luggage, these bags expand with the load. They also don't rust, clank around, and mar floors as metal boxes can.

3. PLASTIC ORGANIZER CASES store and transport fasteners and hardware. Get one with moveable dividers to accommodate different size items. These portable cases are about the size of a small attaché case, with sturdy carrying handles. One type is divided down the middle, and each side is covered with a snap-down clear plastic lid. On one side you can carry an assortment of nails, brads, tacks, and staples; on the other, a variety of screws. For big jobs like framing a dormer or hanging drywall, of course, you'll need to buy fasteners by the pound. But for most small jobs, this kit can hold what you need and make it easy to find.

Organize your tools by task. Equip one small toolbox for electrical work: Include a voltage tester, soldering guns and irons, wire strippers, lineman's pliers, neon test lamp, and the like. Put all your drywall tools in another bag: paintbrushes, caulking gun, paint scrapers, stirring sticks, paint can opener, etc. That way, you can grab what you need and go without having to search through a mismatched collection for the tool appropriate to a specific job.

7

techniques

THESE PAGES SHOW YOU HOW TO MODIFY your home's structure by removing, building, and altering floors and walls, and installing wiring, plumbing, doors, and windows within them. The techniques, tools, and materials involved are fairly standard and will help you complete not only your basement and attic projects but other remodeling projects you may decide to tackle throughout your home in the future.

By becoming familiar with these techniques, you also gain a better understanding of your home. You'll be able to look at your home with X-ray vision: You'll know what lies behind the paint and wallboard and how the space can be modified. You'll also be better able to recognize the potential in an unfinished space and envision the results—a neatly finished, completely equipped, comfortable living area.

OPPOSITE: A staircase with an open banister keeps this basement study from feeling closed. Recessed cans provide general lighting, while recessed spots handle task lighting over the desk—there's no gloom and doom in this basement. A mix of textures—stained wood, painted woodwork, nubby carpet, and denim upholstery—creates a fresh look that's clean and comfortable.

floor techniques

Wood-framed floors, whether they're in an attic or installed over a concrete slab in a basement, consist of the following components:

JOISTS are generally 2×6s that run horizontally across the tops of walls. They make up the structure to which the ceiling of the room beneath is fastened, and they support the floor in a finished attic. In unfinished attics joists may be exposed or covered with insulation.

TOP PLATES are structural elements that form the upper surface of exterior walls. They generally consist of two 2×4s nailed one on top of the other; joists are nailed to these.

RAFTERS, often 2×6s, are structural elements that support a roof. Rafters intersect the top plate at an angle and are fastened to the top plate.

SUBFLOORING, nailed directly to the joists, is the first layer of a finished floor. Most subfloors are made with plywood, oriented strand board (OSB) or, in older construction, diagonally laid planking. If your finished floor will be wood, tile, laminate, or carpet, you can install it directly on top of a smooth plywood subfloor.

UNDERLAYMENT is fastened to the subfloor to provide a smooth, level base over which a resilient floor covering is applied. This extra layer ensures surface imperfections in the subfloor don't telegraph through the flexible finish material.

FLOOR COVERING is the surface of the finished floor. It may be carpet, hardwood, laminate, tile, vinyl, or some other material.

Strengthening a floor's structure

You'll need:

- ■ Tape measure
- ■ Marking pencil
- ■ Circular saw
- ■ Speed square
- ■ Hammer
- ■ Nails

1 **THE FIRST STEP** in finishing an attic is to make sure the joists are strong enough to carry the load of a finished room and its contents. (Attic joists may be sized for ceiling and storage loads only and may not be strong enough to support a living space.) Check with a local code official to see what your local building codes specify. Codes sometimes have different specifications for rooms with different functions.

2 **IF EXISTING JOISTS** aren't strong enough to bear the load, you can strengthen them by adding sister joists—lumber of equal thickness nailed to the face of each existing joist and toenailed to the top plate. If wires or plumbing pierce existing joists, you need to remove and either reinstall or re-route these systems when you add sister joists.

Installing a new subfloor

You'll need:

- ■ Tape measure
- ■ Marking pencil
- ■ Circular saw
- ■ Hammer
- ■ Caulking gun
- ■ Construction adhesive
- ■ 8d ringshank nails
- ■ ⅝–¾-inch CDX plywood

Installing a subfloor

You'll need a helper to assist you in carrying and positioning the plywood sheets, but installation itself moves surprisingly quickly. Work from the room's entry toward the outside walls, so you have installed floor to carry materials over.

1 WHEN FLOOR JOISTS are strong enough to meet code, you're ready to put down a surface. This is a fun, quick, and easy step and, when you're done, the room looks dramatically different. The toughest part is getting the 4×8-foot plywood sheets to the job. Sheets of ⅝–¾-inch CDX plywood are heavy and awkward. Inexpensive carrying handles at home centers make it possible for one strong person to carry the plywood, but you still probably need a helper to maneuver them up the stairs.

2 START INSTALLING the subfloor in the corner nearest your entry, laying down each plywood sheet loosely. Now you'll have something to walk on as you carry in additional sheets. Line up the first sheet at right angles to the joists, square to the room, and with its edge centered on a joist. Fasten it with 8d ringshank nails at 6-inch intervals on the perimeter and at 10-inch intervals within the panel. To eliminate squeaks lay a bead of construction adhesive before nailing. To prevent damage to the ceiling below, use an air nailer or screws instead of hand-nailing. Continue laying sheets until you cover the entire floor. Don't butt sheets against one another—they need an ⅛-inch gap between them to allow for expansion and contraction. Place a couple of 8d nails as spacers between the edge of each new sheet and the sheet adjacent, on all four sides, before nailing. Remove spacer nails when you finish fastening.

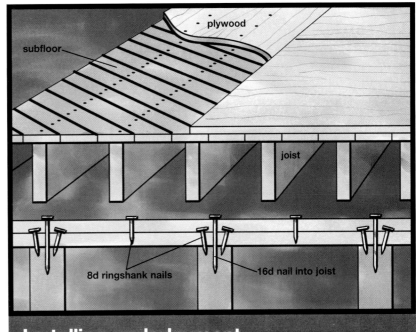

Installing underlayment

When laying ¾-inch plywood underlayment use 8d ringshank nails to fasten it to the plank underlayment between joists, and 16d nails driven through the subfloor and into the joists.

Installing underlayment

You'll need:

- Tape measure
- Marking pencil
- Circular saw
- Hammer
- 8d ringshank nails
- ¼-⅜-inch APA underlayment

1 IF YOU'RE FINISHING your floor with resilient flooring, such as linoleum, cork, or vinyl, add one more layer. This is the underlayment, which keeps imperfections below from telegraphing through to the finished floor surface. Use APA underlayment rated plywood for this purpose. Stagger the joints of these under-layment panels every 4 feet, so the subfloor joints fall in the middle of each sheet of underlayment.

Fasten the underlayment to the subfloor and the floor joists using 8d ringshank and 16d nails, as shown in the illustration *above*.

Underlayment

Don't use just any plywood for underlayment—plywood that has voids and rough surfaces isn't suitable for this application. Instead specify plywood rated by the American Plywood Association (APA) for underlayment use. This plywood has a very high impact load resistance to resist bending and denting. For areas covered by resilient flooring, specify "sanded face" underlayment.

This section focuses on removing and adding wood-framed walls that are not load-bearing. Consult an engineer before attempting to make changes to load-bearing walls, which are much more complicated—they support the weight of your house—and require special techniques. Removing and installing non-load-bearing walls is fairly simple. Behind the drywall or plaster, the walls consist of vertical studs that butt at the top and bottom against horizontal 2×4 pieces called plates.

If your project involves reworking a previous or partially finished space, you may need to remove some existing walls first to prepare the space for your new floor plan. If so follow these steps.

Dust control

You'll need:

- Measuring tape
- Plastic sheeting
- Duct tape
- Spring clamps

1 BEFORE REMOVING WALLS build a curtain of plastic sheeting to enclose your work area. Tape the edges of the plastic to the walls and floor with duct tape to prevent dust from migrating into your living area. Create a makeshift doorway by overlapping the plastic. Leave a 12- to 18-inch gap in the plastic where the doorway will be.

After the plastic is up, slit the sheet vertically to make two flaps. Seal the flaps by folding them together, then clipping them with two or three spring clamps. Place a doormat just outside your makeshift doorway; vacuum it frequently throughout the course of your project. If you're working in a room that has a window, prop a box fan in the opened window so that it blows dust out. No window? Buy a portable HEPA air filter from a home center to catch airborne dust. Position it as close to dusty jobs as is safe and practical, and enjoy cleaner air and less dust throughout the house.

Removing molding and trim

You'll need:

- Utility knife
- Putty knife
- 3-inch drywall knife
- Flat pry bar
- ¼-inch plywood scrap
- Pliers
- End nips

You can reuse molding and trim if they are carefully removed.

1 USE A UTILITY KNIFE to cut through the paint seams that glue moldings to the wall.

2 SLIP A PUTTY KNIFE between an end of the molding and the wall. Tap it gently with a hammer to push it between the wall and molding. Work the knife gently back and forth to loosen the molding.

3 WORK A 3-INCH DRYWALL knife into the crack you formed with the putty knife. Continue to pry gently along the length of the molding until you are able to see the nails fastening the molding in place.

4 USE A FLAT PRY BAR to work the molding loose. As you move along the length, gently pry the area around each nail. Slip a scrap of ¼-inch plywood beneath the bar to avoid damaging the wall or floor.

5 PULL NAILS through the backside of the molding with pliers. Nails won't budge? Clip them off with a pair of end nips, then file them flush to the molding.

Removing drywall

You'll need:

- Plug-in radio
- Screwdriver
- Utility knife
- Hammer
- Flat pry bar
- Dust mask
- Long pants
- Long-sleeved shirt
- Handsaw, reciprocating saw, or saber saw

1 TURN OFF the electrical circuit at the service panel. Sometimes fuses or breakers are labeled according to the circuits they serve.

2 IF YOU FIND LABELS, you still have to test the circuits to make sure you get the right one. Flip a circuit breaker to the off position or remove a fuse. Then plug a radio into each outlet in every receptacle in the

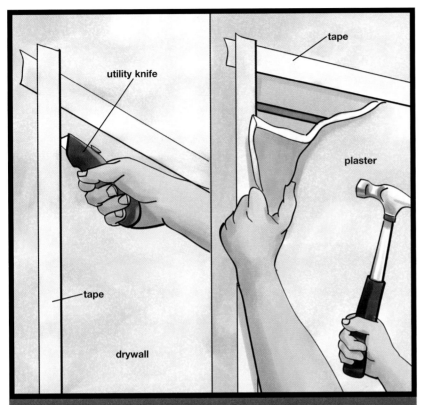

utility knife

tape

tape

plaster

drywall

Removing drywall and plaster

To remove drywall, tape the cutout so the cut will be centered on a stud, then cut through the drywall with a utility knife *above left*. To remove plaster, tape the cutout so the cut is flush with the edge of a stud. Score the plaster on the taped line, then break up the surface with a hammer and remove the pieces. Don't hit the plaster too hard, or you may cause nearby sections of wall to crack.

stud alongside the one you used as a guide; you'll nail the new drywall to it.

5 PUNCH A SERIES of 3- to 4-inch holes in the wall near the ceiling with your hammer.

6 GRASP THE DRYWALL and pull it free from the studs. If necessary slip a flat bar inside the wall and pry drywall from the studs. Break drywall into the largest pieces possible.

7 CLEAN DEBRIS from studs, pulling or unscrewing fasteners as you go. You do this if you plan to reuse the framing and for safe handling if you're going to pitch the material.

8 IF YOU FIND INSULATION in an old wall, reduce skin and lung irritation by wearing a long-sleeve shirt, long pants, and a dust mask when you remove it. Roll insulation and seal it in large plastic garbage bags for disposal.

Removing plaster

You'll need:

- Plug-in radio
- Screwdriver
- Utility knife
- Hammer
- Flat pry bar
- Stud finder
- Handsaw or reciprocating saw
- Dust mask
- Long pants
- Long-sleeve shirt
- 2-inch drywall screws

wall you will work on. If there are switches in the room, test each outlet on each receptacle with the switches in each position to ensure each circuit is dead—sometimes one outlet in a receptacle is controlled by a switch and the other isn't.

3 IF FUSES or breakers aren't labeled, plug a radio into an outlet in the wall to be removed. Turn up the volume loud enough so you can hear it from the service panel. Flip circuit breakers or remove fuses until the radio goes off—you've found the circuit. Label it at the service panel.

Now test each outlet, as described in preceding steps.

4 REMOVE SWITCH and outlet plates. Put on a dust mask that's rated for fine dust. Run a utility knife firmly down both corners of the wall to make a clean break with the wall that's staying in place. If you're removing just part of the wall, establish a break line by cutting the drywall along a stud with a handsaw, reciprocating saw, or saber saw. (Have a helper hold a shop vacuum hose near the saw to pick up dust.) After the wall is down, screw a new

1 TURN OFF the electricity and remove switch and outlet plates

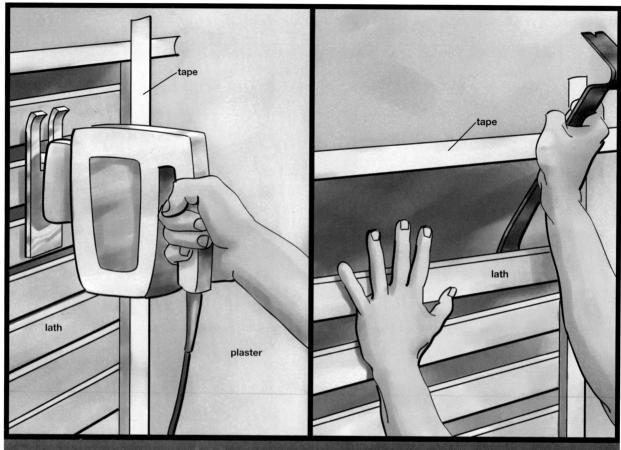

Removing lath

Once you've removed the plaster, use a saber saw, handsaw, or reciprocating saw to cut the lath flush with the adjoining stud. Then use a flat pry bar to remove the lath from the wall cavity.

as described in "Removing drywall" on page 118.

2 ATTACH 1×2s with screws at the intersecting points of the wall you are removing and the adjacent ceiling and other walls to prevent damage to those surfaces that you want to retain intact. (When you're done with the demolition, you'll remove these boards and putty up the screw holes.)

3 PLAN TO END THE DEMOLITION at a stud that will remain in place. Trying to cut into a plaster wall anywhere but adjacent to a stud edge

disrupts the metal mesh or thin strips of wood lath to which the plaster is attached and destroys the plaster. Use a stud finder to locate a stud.

4 KNOCK PLASTER OFF the wall with a hammer. Shovel up the loose plaster debris before you start pulling off the lath behind it. If the lath strips continue past the end stud, cut them flush to the side of the stud with a handsaw, reciprocating saw, or saber saw.

5 REMOVE THE LATH with a flat pry bar, and pile it neatly in an out-of-the-way corner of your work

area for disposal later. For safety reasons pull any nails that remain in the studs or lath as you go.

Removing electrical wiring

You'll need:

- Screwdriver
- Pencil and paper
- Flat pry bar

1 CHECK each outlet to make sure the power is off (see page 119–120).

2 UNSCREW RECEPTACLES and switches; pull them from boxes. Make a sketch of the wire connections. Note which color wire attaches to which terminal.

3 DETACH RECEPTACLES and switches from wires by loosening terminal screws.

4 PULL WIRES out of the boxes, and through any holes in the framing. Unscrew boxes from studs.

5 RUN WIRES back into now-loose boxes, and reattach them as they were to the various switches and receptacles.

6 SCREW DEVICES back into their boxes and replace the cover plates. Now you have removed all the wiring, along with the boxes and receptacles they serve, from the demolished wall. Store them out of the way of your work. When you finish framing new walls, you can rerun the same cable.

Remove framing

You'll need:

- ■ Reciprocating saw
- ■ Hammer
- ■ Flat pry bar
- ■ Handsaw

1 CUT THROUGH NAILS that fasten studs to plates using a reciprocating saw with a metal-cutting blade.

2 REMOVE EACH STUD by knocking it sideways at the bottom with a hammer; then twist and lever the stud free of nails that hold it to top plate. Reuse studs, clearly marking

any embedded nails so you don't ruin a saw blade trying to cut across nails.

3 CUT BOTTOM and top plates free from the portion of the wall that will stay, if they are part of a longer wall. Avoid marring the ceiling and finished floor as you complete the cuts.

4 REMOVE TOP PLATE by driving a flat pry bar between the two layers and prying off the bottom layer. If you're removing a partition wall, the upper top plate overlaps the lower top plate of the main wall. Use a handsaw or reciprocating saw to cut off the top plate at the main wall. If joists run across the wall you're

removing, they are probably nailed to the top plate. Drive a flat pry bar between each joist and the top plate, and pry the top plate free.

5 REMOVE BOTTOM PLATE by prying it free with a flat pry bar.

6 TO REMOVE DOOR framing, cut nails at the bottom of one of the two sets of doubled studs the same way you did for single framing studs. Lever that leg of the doorway free of the bottom plate. Knock doubled studs sideways with your hammer to free them from the header—the piece of framing that runs across the top of the doorway—and the top plate. Pry the header free of remaining studs.

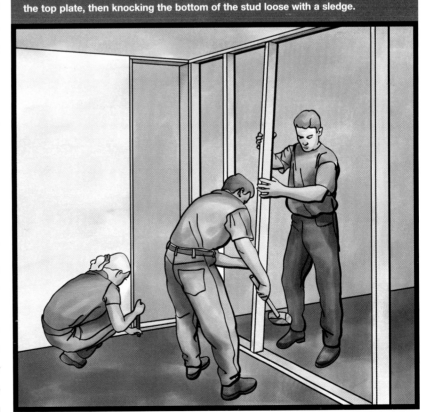

Removing wall studs
After you've bared the wall studs, remove them by twisting the stud loose from the top plate, then knocking the bottom of the stud loose with a sledge.

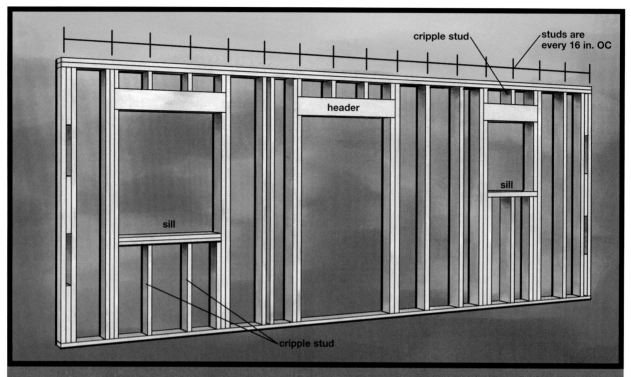

cripple stud

studs are every 16 in. OC

header

sill

sill

cripple stud

Wall framing

New walls are framed with 2×4 or 2×6 studs located every 16 inches on center. Headers frame the tops of openings, jack and king studs frame the sides, and sills define the bottom of an opening. Short cripple studs fill in above and below openings.

Building a wall on the floor

You'll need:

- Hammer
- Tape measure
- Marking pencil
- Plumb bob
- Chalk line
- Chalk
- Nails
- 2½-inch drywall screws
- Shims
- Concrete nails or construction adhesive

1 IF YOU HAVE enough space and a flat floor (and if your house is true and square), build your wall on the floor, then tip it up into place. That way you nail through the bottom and top plates directly into the bottom and top of the studs, which is easier than toenailing (driving nails at an angle through the sides of the stud and into the plate).

2 NAIL A TOP PLATE to the ceiling where you want to position your wall. This allows you to build the wall 1½ inches short, which allows you to tip the wall up, slide it into place under this second plate, and attach it with ease. (Full-height walls get hung up on the ceiling when they're tipped into position.) Work in 16-foot sections when building long walls.

Kings, jacks, and cripples

Several bits of archaic terminology define lumber framing. Here are some common terms defined:

PLATE: A horizontal framing member that runs across the top or bottom of a wall

STUD: A vertical framing member

KING: A stud that frames a doorway opening and runs from the top plate to the bottom plate

JACK: A stud that frames a doorway opening and runs from the header to the bottom plate

HEADER: A horizontal framing member that runs across the top of a door or window opening

CRIPPLE: A stud that does not span the entire height of a wall, such as those that run between a header and the top plate

3 MEASURE FROM the underside of the ceiling plate to the floor to determine the wall height. Check in several places and use the smallest dimension as the height.

4 CUT PLATES and studs to length. Make studs 3 inches shorter than the wall height you determined. This allows for the thickness of two 2×4 plates (1½ inches each). If you are running wiring through the wall, stack up the studs that the wire will run through, clamp them together, ends flush, and drill through them all at once with a ¾-inch spade or auger bit. Now you

won't have to drill individual holes.

5 MARK PLATES for stud centers by holding plates side by side. Hook your tape over one end and stretch it out, making a mark every 16 inches. Measure ¾ inch on either side of each mark and draw lines to show where the sides of the studs will be.

6 PLACE STUDS on edge between plates; then nail them into place. Make sure stud edges are flush with plate edges.

7 MARK THE WALL location on the floor by dangling a plumb bob from the end of the ceiling plate

to the floor. Repeat at the other end. If you're working alone, hang a plump bob from a nail in the plate.

8 POSITION WALL so bottom plate is a foot away from the chalk line. Lift wall by the top plate and tip it up until it's vertical. Slide it into position under ceiling plate.

9 SHIM THE WALL. If there's space between the top plate and the ceiling plate, slip some shims between the two.

10 ANCHOR THE WALL by nailing up through the top plate into the ceiling plate. If you use shims, drive the nails through the shims to secure them. Make sure the edges of the two plates are flush. To protect a plaster ceiling, install the plate with 3-inch-long drywall screws instead of nails. Check wall for plumb with a carpenter's level, then nail the bottom plate to the floor. If you're building on concrete, secure the bottom plate with 2-inch masonry nails or a ½-inch bead of construction adhesive. Masonry nails are cheaper and less messy; construction adhesive is the way to go if your concrete is too hard to nail into.

Building a wall in place

You'll need:
- All items mentioned in previous section
- Drill and drill bit

Build your wall in place if you're

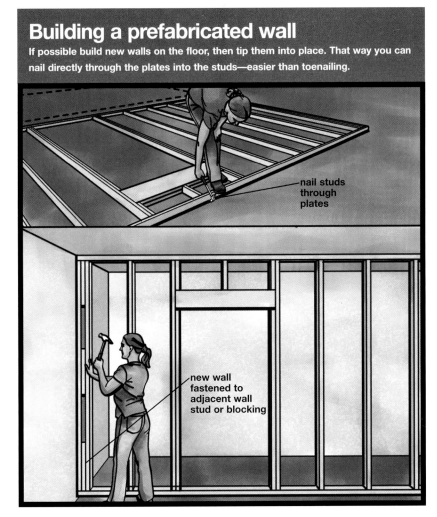

Building a prefabricated wall
If possible build new walls on the floor, then tip them into place. That way you can nail directly through the plates into the studs—easier than toenailing.

nail studs through plates

new wall fastened to adjacent wall stud or blocking

Typical residential doors measure 32 inches wide and 80 inches tall, so rough openings should be 34 inches wide and 82 inches tall. Don't rely on these dimensions, though. Purchase (or at least measure) the door you're installing before framing its opening. If you're in doubt about how big to make the opening, make it ¼ inch on the larger side. You can always use shims to make a too-small door fit, but a door that's too big for its opening is a nuisance to cut down. Doors are available in many sizes, so if a 32-inch door doesn't work for you, ask your supplier what else is available.

Framing a doorway

You'll need:

- ■ Tape measure
- ■ Speed square
- ■ Circular saw
- ■ Hammer
- ■ 16d nails
- ■ 10d nails
- ■ 0d nails
- ■ Carpenter's level
- ■ Handsaw

Building a wall in place

Mark the ceiling joists for the location of the top plate; mark ceiling joist locations on top plate. Nail through the plate into the joists.

working in tight quarters or an older house that's no longer square and true. Start by laying out the plates, as described previously. Attach the wall top plate to the plate already attached to the ceiling. Use a plumb bob to locate the bottom plate. Anchor it to the floor. Cut studs to fit in between plates. Toenail them in place top and bottom. Pre-drill holes to simplify nail driving.

About rough openings

Rough openings are the spaces made for a door or a window in a wall. For a door a rough opening is usually 2 inches wider and taller than the door size, not including the jambs. This allows space for the jambs that make the finished opening plus a little extra for shimming the assembly should the opening not be exactly plumb.

Position walls for easy construction

In the best situations, walls are attached to joists. Walls installed perpendicular to joists are easier to build because you can nail their top plates through the ceiling into the joists. If your new wall will run parallel to joists, adjust the floor plan so the wall falls directly under a joist. If that's not possible, you need to open the ceiling to install blocking to which the top plate can be attached. If you're attaching a top plate through a plaster ceiling into joists, pre-drill the plate and attach it with 2½-inch drywall screws (avoid hammering, which can damage the ceiling).

1 FRAMING A DOORWAY is easier to do while the wall is flat on the floor. Lay out positions of jack and king studs simultaneously on the two plates. These studs define the sides of a rough opening.

2 PREPARE TO make partial cuts in the bottom plate. You do this to establish the width of the rough opening and to make the portion of the plate that now runs through the bottom of the door opening easier to remove later. Set a circular saw to make a cut $1\frac{1}{8}$ inches deep. Cut across the bottom plate on the waste side of the lines.

3 NAIL JACK AND KING studs in place. Cut jack studs to rough opening height, and nail them to the bottom plate with 16d nails, to sides of king studs with 10d nails.

4 MAKE A HEADER for the door's top opening from doubled 2x4s nailed together with 10d nails. Install header with two 16d nails through each king stud.

5 NAIL A CRIPPLE to each king stud with 10d nails to hold header firmly to jack studs. Attach them to the top plate with 16d nails. Cripples continue the 16-inch on-center spacing of the wall studs. Attach them with 16d nails through top plate and 8d toenails into header.

6 INSTALL THE WALL. Make sure sides of the opening are plumb. Cut away the bottom plate portion that spans the doorway. Use a handsaw to finish cuts. Don't cut into the floor on either side of the doorway.

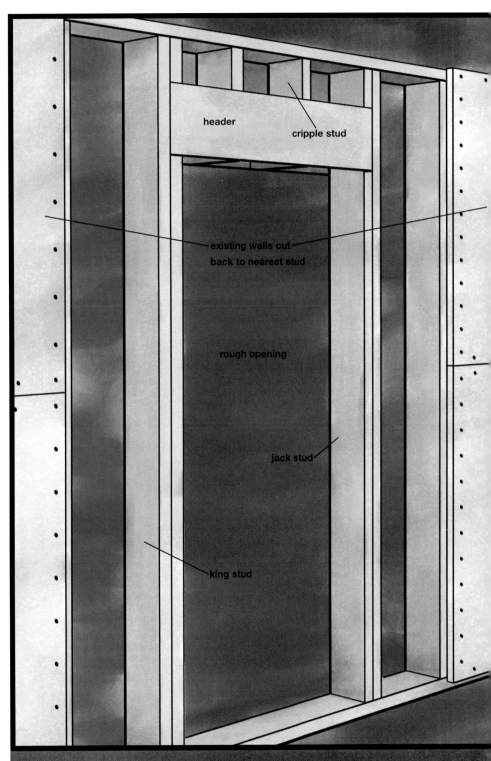

header

cripple stud

existing walls cut back to nearest stud

rough opening

jack stud

king stud

Cutting a rough opening
To create a new rough opening, cut back existing wall to nearest studs. Install new jack studs, king studs, header, cripple studs, and sill. Cut the sill after the wall is up.

wiring
techniques

After you remove unnecessary walls and frame in new walls, it's time to run electrical wiring before adding insulation and drywall. The following sections introduce you to the basic components of house wiring before showing you how to install wiring in your new space.

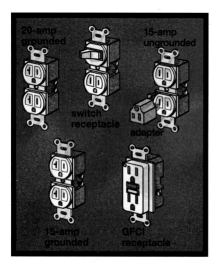

Receptacles

Duplex receptacles have two outlets for receiving plugs. Each outlet has a long (neutral) slot, a shorter (hot) slot, and a half-round grounding hole, which ensures that the plug is polarized and grounded. Receptacles are rated for maximum amps. A 20-amp grounded receptacle has a T-shape neutral slot; use it only on 20-amp circuits. For most purposes a 15-amp grounded receptacle suffices; a 20-amp single-grounded receptacle makes overloading a critical circuit nearly impossible.

Ungrounded receptacles are intended only for use in older homes where circuits lack ground wires.

Combination switch/receptacles have switches that can be hooked up to control the receptacles they're paired with.

GFCI (ground fault circuit interrupter) receptacles must be used when an outlet is located within 6 feet of a water fixture. The GFCI is a safety device that shuts down a circuit or receptacle when it senses a shock hazard.

Wire

Wire, cord, and cable—the conductors—provide the routes along which electricity travels.

Wire is a solid strand of metal wrapped in insulation; cord is a group of small metal strands wrapped in insulation; and cable is made of two or more wires encased in protective sheathing of metal or plastic.

Flexible armored cable (BX) contains wires wrapped in a flexible metal sheathing. Wire gauge, or size, determines how much electrical current the wire can carry. For instance, 14-gauge wire carries a maximum of 15 amps, 12-gauge wire carries up to 20 amps, and 10-gauge wire carries up to 30 amps.

The coding printed on sheathing

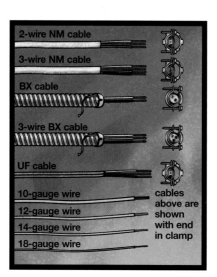

tells you what's inside. For example, 14-2 G cable has two 14-gauge wires inside plus a bare ground wire (G stands for ground).

Switches

Single-pole toggle switches turn lights and receptacles on and off. Most home electrical switches are this type.

Three-way or four-way switches allow you to control a light from two or three separate switch locations.

Rocker switches function like standard toggles but are slightly easier to use, as you simply press one side of the

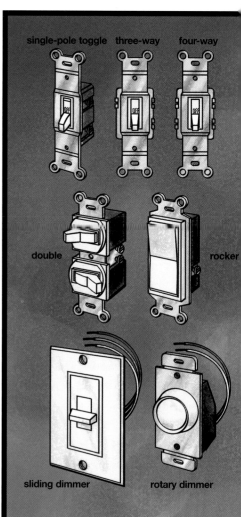

Wire savvy

COLOR	FUNCTION
white	neutral, carries power back to service panel
black	hot, carries power from service panel
red, other colors	also hot, color-coded to help identify which circuit it's on
white with black tape	a white wire being used as a hot wire
bare or green	a ground wire

rocker to switch on, the other side to switch off.

Dimmer switches allow you to adjust light levels.

Stripping wire

You'll need:

- Cable ripper
- Side-cutting pliers
- Combination tool or adjustable stripper

1 TO MAKE ELECTRICAL connections, remove some of the sheathing that encases the three or four wires of the cable and strip some of the insulation that covers the individual wires. Doing so enables the metal part of the wire that carries the current to make contact with the terminal or wire that it's being attached to. Stripping wire is a simple job, but it must be done with great care, or you can end up with dangerous electrical shorts.

If you think you've damaged a wire's insulation by slicing into it accidentally, cut back the cable to a place behind the damaged spot and start again. Strip wires before, rather than after, the cable is pulled into the box, so if you do make a mistake you can cut off the damaged portion of the wire and try again.

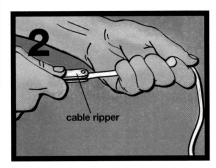

2 REMOVE PLASTIC SHEATHING from nonmetallic sheathed cable with a cable ripper. Slip 6 to 8 inches of cable into the ripper's jaws, squeeze, and pull. This slits the sheathing without damaging the insulation of internal wires.

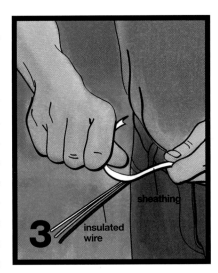

3 PEEL BACK THE SHEATHING you slit as well as any paper wrapping or strips of thin plastic. You'll find two or three separately insulated wires and a bare ground wire.

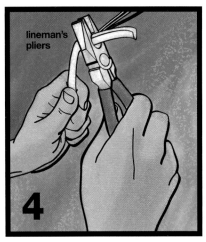

4 CUT OFF sheathing and paper with a pair of lineman's pliers.

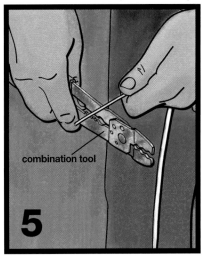

5 STRIP INSULATION from the wires with a combination tool, which has separate holes for different wire sizes. Place wire in the correct holes, clamp down, give the wire a twist, and pull the tool away from you. Use the same technique used with an adjustable stripper; after it's set for correct wire size, you don't have to look for the right hole every time.

Working with wire

You'll need:

- ■ Wire connectors
- ■ Soldering iron or gun
- ■ Lead-free, rosin-core solder
- ■ Electrical tape
- ■ Side-cutting pliers
- ■ Combination tool
- ■ Needle-nose pliers
- ■ Screwdriver

The most satisfying phase of an electrical installation comes when you tie the wires together and attach them to switches, light fixtures, and receptacles. It is extremely important to refrain from taking shortcuts. Never overcrowd a box with more wires than your local electrical code allows.

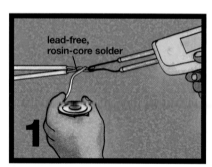

lead-free, rosin-core solder

1 USE WIRE CONNECTORS to splice wires. They come in a variety of sizes and are color-coded to help decipher how many wires of what thickness can be used with them (see chart *right*). Don't depend on the connector to do the joining—twist the wires firmly together first, then twist on the wire connector, turning it by hand until it tightens firmly. Make sure no bare wires show

where they enter the connector. Some codes require splices to be soldered. More often, however, the soldering of house wiring is prohibited. If you need to solder a splice, start by twisting the wires together. Heat the wires with a soldering iron or gun, then touch solder to the splice. The solder melts into the splice. Insulate soldered splices by wrapping them with electrical tape, covering bare wire ends, and overlapping the wire insulation with tape by an inch or so.

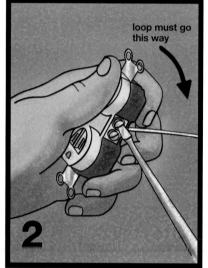

loop must go this way

2 CONNECT A WIRE to a terminal by stripping just enough wire to wrap around the terminal, about ¾ inch. Then form the wire into a loop using needle-nose or lineman's pliers. You may need a little practice to make correctly sized loops that lie

flat. Hook the wire clockwise around the terminal so that the loop closes when screws are tightened. With receptacles black wires go to the brass side, white wires go to silver. Tighten firmly but avoid overtightening, which can crack the device. If the device suffers damage, throw it out.

3 IF YOU MUST join multiple wires to a terminal, make a pigtail: Cut a short piece of wire (about 4 inches), strip both ends, and splice it to the other wires with a wire nut (or solder them, if your codes require it). Then attach the free end of the pigtail to the appropriate terminal. (Never attach more than one wire to a terminal. Codes prohibit it, and it's unsafe—terminal screws are made to hold only one wire.)

4 GROUND ALL RECEPTACLES and switches. When you use flexible armored cable (BX), Greenfield, or rigid conduit, the metal of the wiring casing and the metal of the box substitute for

How many wires can a connector hold?

CONNECTOR COLOR	12-GAUGE WIRE	14-GAUGE WIRE
red	2–4	2–5
yellow	2–3	2–4
orange	2	2–4

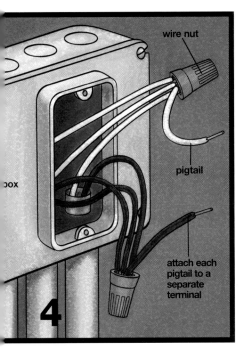

4

wire nut

pigtail

attach each pigtail to a separate terminal

box

Wiring a new wall

You'll need:

- Electric drill
- ¾-inch spade or auger bit
- Wire staples
- Metal plates
- Hammer
- Nails
- Conduit
- Screws
- Masonry anchors

1

the grounding wire. The simple act of firmly attaching the metal wire casing to the box grounds it. Some local codes require you to attach a short grounding wire as well. If you're working with nonmetallic sheathed cable (Romex) and metal boxes, connect short ground wires to the box and device. With nonmetallic boxes the cable's ground wire connects directly to the device.

1 **FOR HORIZONTAL RUNS** through studs, drill ¾-inch holes in the studs with a spade or auger bit; then feed the wires through. Although you can do this after the wall is framed, it is easier if you know where the wires go before assembling the wall. After the studs have been cut, but before they've been nailed to the plates, clamp the studs together, ends flush, and drill through all the studs at once. That way, you know that the holes all line up, and you don't have to measure and drill a sep-

arate hole in each one once the wall is assembled. To avoid weakening the lumber, drill holes at least 1¼ inches from the face edge of the stud. Install a metal plate over the stud if the hole must be made less than 1¼ inches from the edge. Doing so prevents you from driving a nail or screw into the wire when hanging a picture or shelf bracket.

2 **FOR VERTICAL RUNS,** staple wire loosely along the wide face of a stud with wire staples.

3 **FOR RUNS THROUGH PLATES** and joists, drill near walls, if

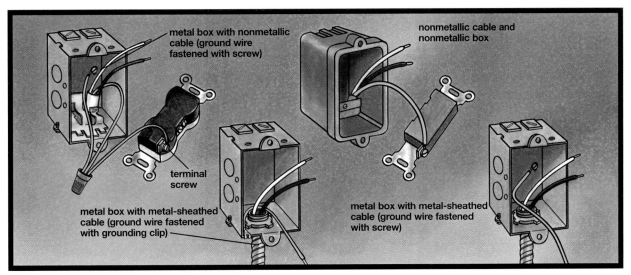

metal box with nonmetallic cable (ground wire fastened with screw)

nonmetallic cable and nonmetallic box

terminal screw

metal box with metal-sheathed cable (ground wire fastened with grounding clip)

metal box with metal-sheathed cable (ground wire fastened with screw)

possible. Drill holes 2 inches from the faces of joists.

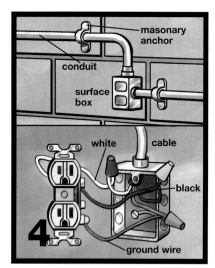

masonary anchor

conduit

surface box

white   cable

black

ground wire

4 **FOR INSTALLATIONS** on concrete walls, use surface-mount boxes. Run wires through conduit that's anchored to the wall with brackets, screws, and masonry anchors, as shown.

Running circuits

You'll need:

- Electric drill
- ¾-inch spade or auger bit
- Mason's line
- Weight
- Fish tape

Basements are fairly easy to wire because wiring is exposed in unfinished ceilings and new circuits can be added without having to fish wires.

Attics are a bit more complex, especially if they are already finished, but hardly problematic.

1 **CHOOSE AN ENTRY POINT** that's directly above an outlet in a

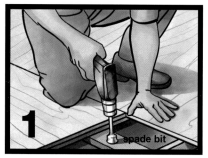

spade bit

lower-story wall for the new circuit. Drill a ¾-inch hole through the top plate of the attic wall at that location.

2 **FIND THE CIRCUIT** in the basement that feeds the outlet and drill up 4 inches to either side of the wire.

hole for cable to attic

3 **DROP A WEIGHTED MASON'S** line or small chain from the hole in the attic; pull it through the outlet hole. Feed a fish tape from the basement and tie it to the line. Attach the cable to the fish tape; pull the line up with the fish tape and cable attached.

mason's line

Tapping into existing lines

You'll need:

- ■ Tape measure
- ■ Marking pencil
- ■ Straightedge
- ■ Reciprocating saw or drywall saw and hacksaw
- ■ Pipe and fittings
- ■ Pipe primer and cement (if working with plastic pipe)
- ■ Propane torch with soldering tip (if working with copper pipe)
- ■ Pipe flux and solder (if working with copper pipe)

When it comes to plumbing, it's worth hiring a professional, especially if your home is older or has cast-iron pipe. Cast iron is heavy and can shatter into sharp edges. Some plumbers may be willing to make only the cast-iron connections; you can save money by making the plastic connections yourself. Similarly you may want a pro to tap into the main stack for a new vent, leaving only the new drain and supply projects for you (see pages 132–133).

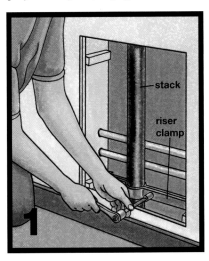

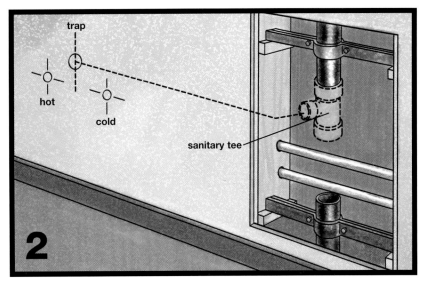

1 SHUT OFF WATER and drain lines. Cut open the wall that contains plumbing to the center of a stud (on either side) so you'll have a nailing surface for patching later. You may have to make a separate hole to access supply pipes. Anchor the stack by attaching riser clamps above and below the section you will be cutting.

2 LAY OUT ROUGH-IN dimensions for the fixture and mark them on wall framing. Be sure the location of the fixture doesn't exceed the maximum distance from the stack allowed by local codes. To determine at which point the fixture ties into the stack, draw a line that slopes from the center of the drain trap at ¼ inch per foot. Cutting squarely, use a hacksaw or reciprocating saw to remove a section of stack that's 8 inches longer than the sanitary tee you're installing.

3 FIT THE SANITARY TEE, two spacers, and two slip couplings into place. Slide couplings up and down to secure spacers. Simply dry-

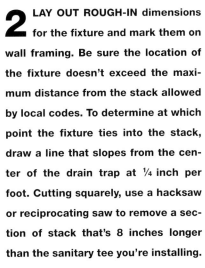

fit pieces at this point; don't cement them until the run of plumbing is complete.

4 NOTCH STUDS just deep enough to support the pipes. (Deep notches weaken wall studs.) In most cases a 45-degree elbow and a short spacer at the stack, and a 90-degree elbow and a trap adapter at the trap, work best. After you're sure the pipe slopes at ¼ inch per foot, scribe all the pieces with alignment marks, disassemble, prime, and cement the plastic drainpipe pieces

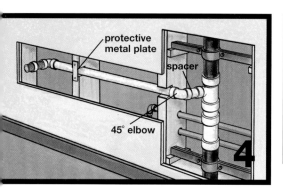

protective metal plate

spacer

45° elbow

4

together (see instructions on pages 134–135).

spacer

5

5 TAP INTO COPPER OR PLASTIC supply lines using spacers, slip couplings, and tees similar to those on the drainpipe. (For soldering copper joints, see pages 136–137). If you tap into galvanized-steel supply lines, you may have to remove sections of pipe and install unions. Use transition fittings when connecting different pipe materials. When making a transition from steel pipe to copper pipe, use a special dielectric fitting, or the joint will corrode.

6 RUN PIPES to fixture locations using 90-degree elbows and pipe, as needed. Use 90-degree

rag to seal off sewer gas

6 caps to seal supply lines temporarily

elbows and short pieces to bring lines beyond the wall surface. Stuff a rag in the drain to seal off sewer gas (it smells bad and can be toxic). Solder caps on the ends of supply lines (see pages 136–137), turn on the water, and test for leaks. To eliminate the possibility of poking a hole in a pipe when nailing up drywall, protect drainpipes by installing a metal nail plate over notches in the studs. Then turn off the water again, add stop valves, and install the fixture.

Running drain lines

You'll need:

- Tape measure
- Marking pencil
- Straightedge
- Hacksaw
- Utility knife
- Pipe and fittings
- Pipe primer and cement

Cutting, moving, and refitting plastic pipe are simple jobs for novice plumbers to take on, as long as you have a plastic waste stack and easy access to the drainpipe. Every drain line must be properly vented. Plan for this before you start cutting drainpipe. You

may need to tap in at a second, higher point for the vent.

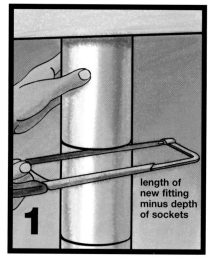

length of new fitting minus depth of sockets

1

1 MEASURE THE new sanitary tee to see how much of the old pipe you need to remove, and subtract the depth of its sockets so the pipe has adequate length to fit solidly inside the tee. Be sure both sides of existing pipe are supported so they stay in position after the cut is made. Cut with a hacksaw; remove burrs with a knife. Or use a no-hub connector.

2 INSTALL THE TOP END of the sanitary tee, then the bottom.

2

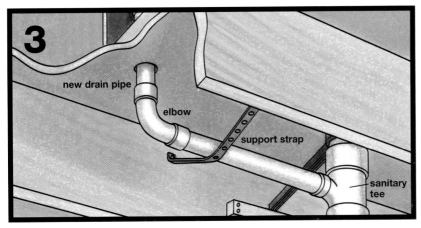

new drain pipe

elbow

support strap

sanitary tee

You may have to loosen some of the support straps to provide enough play in the pipes to do this. After the sanitary tee is dry-fit in desired position, make an alignment mark.

3 RUN PIPES to new fixture's location. If you need to run drainpipe through wall plates or framing, cut holes to accommodate the pipe. Leave at least ⅝ inch of wood on any side that will receive drywall, so nails or screws driven through drywall and into the plate won't pierce the pipe. Connect the drainpipe to the sanitary tee with elbows and lengths of pipe. Dry-fit pieces, draw alignment lines, disassemble, prime, and cement pieces together (see pages 134–135). Support each horizontal pipe run with at least one strap.

Running supply lines

You'll need:

- Tape measure
- Marking pencil
- Straightedge
- Reciprocating saw or drywall saw and hacksaw
- Pipe and fittings
- Pipe primer and cement (if working with plastic pipe)
- Propane torch with soldering tip (if working with copper pipe)
- Pipe flux and solder (if working with copper pipe)

Extending supply lines to meet a sink's new location is a relatively easy job. Turn off water and drain lines. If you're tapping into old galvanized pipe, open it at a convenient union and dismantle it back to the nearest fitting. Or tee-in the supply by cutting a supply pipe and removing both ends.

1 USE A DIELECTRIC ADAPTER if you're going from galvanized to copper or plastic pipe (check local code to be sure plastic is allowed). Never hook copper pipe directly to

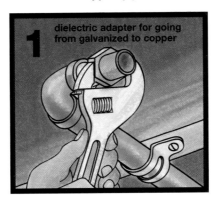

dielectric adapter for going from galvanized to copper

galvanized pipe. A reactive process, called electrolytic action, corrodes the connection.

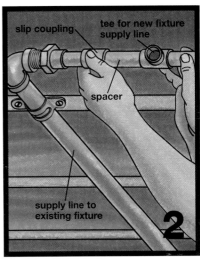

slip coupling

tee for new fixture supply line

spacer

supply line to existing fixture

2 REPLACE THE GALVANIZED pipe run with copper or plastic pipe and a tee fitting. Splice with a slip coupling and spacer. Solder or cement the pipes and fittings. Install pipes that lead to the new fixture, slightly sloping the lines so the system easily drains.

3 USE DROP Ls instead of regular elbows at the new fixture. Attach them with screws to wood that's firmly anchored to framing.

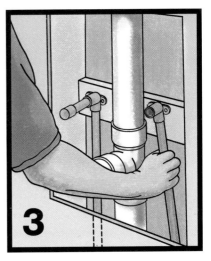

Position Ls 6 to 8 inches apart. Cap the lines, turn on the water, and check for leaks. Don't finish the wall until the building inspector has inspected the pipes.

Installing stop valves

You'll need:

- ■ Stop valves
- ■ Flexible plastic or copper lines
- ■ Thread-sealing tape
- ■ Two adjustable wrenches

Any time a waterline bursts or a faucet needs repair, you'll be grateful to have a stop valve on each individual fixture. With stop valves in place, you can work on a fixture without cutting off water supply to the whole house. Sinks require a stop valve on both the hot and cold lines. Stop valves are made for all pipe and material sizes. For copper lines use brass valves; galvanized and plastic pipes take steel and plastic stop valves, respectively. If the valve will be in view, choose one with an attractive chrome finish. Use flexible copper or plastic line to make a connection from a stop valve to a sink.

thread-sealing tape for threaded pipe

Working with rigid plastic pipe

You'll need:

- ■ Tape measure
- ■ Hacksaw
- ■ Miter box
- ■ Pipe and fittings
- ■ Pipe primer and cement

Do-it-yourself plumbers like plastic pipe because it's inexpensive and fairly easy to work with, it goes together without any special tools or techniques, and it can be cut with a hacksaw. You can easily smooth burrs from the fresh-cut plastic with a utility knife, prime the pipe, and glue parts together.

The most critical aspects of using plastic pipe are the preplanning and attention to detail required, as well as a willingness to do things in a strict order. If you make a mistake, parts can't be taken apart; you simply have to cut out the faulty section, throw it away, and start over.

Several types of plastic pipe exist; check local codes to be sure you use the right type for your job. In most places either ABS or PVC are accepted (and sometimes required) for drain lines. Many localities don't allow plastic pipe for supply lines; others specify CPVC. Don't mix ABS with PVC. Each expands and contracts at different rates, and each uses a specific type of cement that must be used to join them. Plastic pipe is not as stiff as metal pipe, so it requires additional support. Secure horizontal runs with appropriate hangers spaced every 4 to 5 feet.

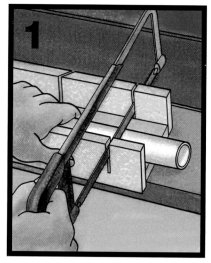

1 MEASURE PIPE for cutting. Ensure a solid fit by adding the depth of a fitting's socket to the pipe's length. Cut pipe in a miter box using a hack saw, back saw, or any fine-tooth saw. Use a straight cut; diagonal cuts reduce the amount of bonding area at the deepest part of the fitting's socket—the most critical part of the joint.

2 REMOVE BURRS from the pipe's cut end (both inside and out) with a sharp utility knife. When pipe is pushed into the fitting, burrs

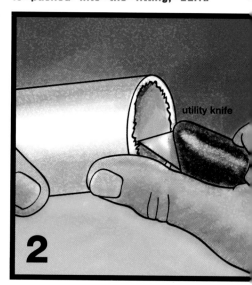

utility knife

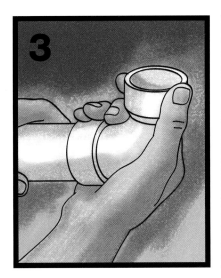

3

scrape away cement and seriously weaken the bond.

3 DRY-FIT THE CONNECTION. Pipe must enter at least one-third of the way into the fitting. If the pipe feels loose, try another fitting. Unlike copper components, plastic pipes and fittings are designed with tapered walls on the inside of the socket, so the pipe makes contact well before it reaches the socket shoulder.

4 CEMENT PIECES together. You have less than a minute to position the pipe and fitting before cement sets. Draw an alignment mark across the pipe and fitting of each joint. When you fit pieces together, you'll know exactly how to position them.

5 WIPE A fitting's pipe end with a clean cloth inside and out.

6 COAT THE OUTSIDE of the pipe end with a special primer if you are working with PVC or CPVC (but not ABS). Many inspectors require purple-colored primer so they can see that joints have been properly primed.

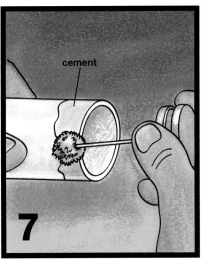

cement

7

7 SWAB A SMOOTH COATING of cement (designed for your type of plastic) onto the pipe end immediately after you prime it.

8 REPEAT THE PROCESS on the inside of the fitting. Apply cement generously but don't let it puddle. Reapply a coating of cement to the pipe end.

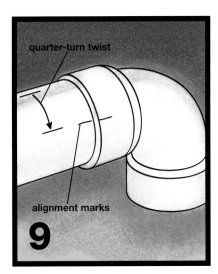

quarter-turn twist

alignment marks

9

9 PUSH THE TWO PIECES together forcefully to ensure the pipe moves fully into the socket. Twist a quarter-turn as you push to help spread the cement evenly. Keep

twisting until alignment marks come together. Hold the pipe and fitting together for about 20 seconds to allow them to fuse into a single piece. Wipe away any excess cement.

10 SAW OFF any connection you misalign with a square cut; then install a new fitting with a spacer and slip coupling.

11 CEMENTED JOINTS are strong enough to handle after only 15 minutes, but don't run water in the line for about 2 hours after you assemble it.

Working with rigid copper pipe

You'll need:

■ Tape measure
■ Marking pencil
■ Tubing cutter
■ Emery cloth, steel wool, or wire brush
■ Pipe and fittings
■ Propane torch with soldering tip
■ Pipe flux and solder
■ Sheet metal or cookie sheet

Learning how to solder pipe may be daunting at first but, with practice, it's faster than screwing pipe together. With soldering, sometimes called sweating, molten solder flows into a fitting via capillary action. Just as a blotter soaks up ink, a joint absorbs molten solder, making a watertight bond as strong as the pipe itself.

Open every faucet on the run before soldering so heat and steam from the torch can escape. Otherwise the heat may burn out washers and other parts, and built-up steam may rupture a fitting or even burst through a pipe wall in extreme cases.

1 CUT COPPER PIPE with a tubing cutter. Clamp the cutter onto the tubing, rotate a few times, tighten, and rotate some more. After several repetitions of this process, the pipe will be cut cleanly.

2 REMOVE BURRS on the inside of the pipe you just cut by inserting the reaming blade of a tubing cutter and twisting it.

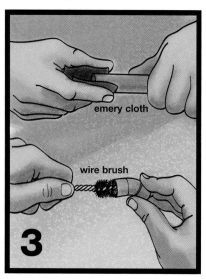

3 GREASE, dirt, and rust can impede the flow of solder. Remove them from the pipe's inside and out with emery cloth, steel wool, or a wire brush. Polish the metal until it is shiny, then avoid touching the polished surfaces. Oil from your fingers can interfere with solder and cause a leak.

4 DRY-FIT PIPE PIECES and fittings to make sure they're the correct length. If you have trouble pushing pieces together, the pipe may have been squeezed out of shape when it was cut. Discard the misshapen pipe and cut a new piece. After you are satisfied with the way everything fits together, take the pieces apart and set them on a clean, dry surface.

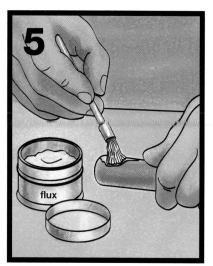

5 BRUSH ON FLUX (also called soldering paste) in a light, even coating to both surfaces you intend to join. Flux retards oxidation when copper is heated. As solder flows into the joint, flux burns away. Use rosin-type flux, not the acid type.

6 PROTECT FLAMMABLE surfaces. If you're working near wood framing, paper-sheathed insulation, or other flammable materials, shield them from the propane torch flame with an old cookie sheet or piece of sheet metal.

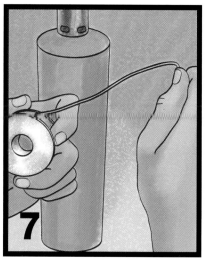

7 UNWIND ABOUT 10 INCHES of solder, straighten it, and bend 2 inches at a 60-degree angle (enough so that it's easy to work with but long enough to keep your fingers away from the flame). Light the torch. Adjust flame until its inner (blue)

cone is about 2 inches long.

heat the fitting, not the joint

8 ASSEMBLE THE CONNECTION and heat the middle of the fitting—not the joint—with the inner cone of the flame. Touch solder to joint. If the joint is hot enough, capillary action pulls solder into joint. Remove flame when solder drips from pipe.

rag is damp, not wet

9 LIGHTLY BRUSH THE JOINT with a damp rag to keep pipes looking neat. Take care not to burn your fingers.

10 TEST THE SYSTEM after you finish installing a new run. Turn on the water supply. If you find a leak, shut off the water, drain the line, and disassemble the joint by heating both sides of the fitting (but

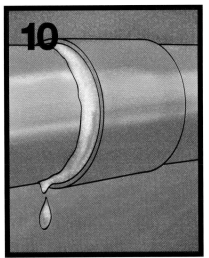

not the soldered joint itself) with a soldering torch's 2-inch-long blue flame. When the pipe is hot, grasp the fitting and pipe with pliers, and pull the joint apart. Remove old solder by heating the pipe end and quickly, carefully wiping it with a dry rag. Let the pipe cool, then polish the end with emery cloth. You can reuse pipe but not fittings; only new fittings provide a watertight seal.

11 SUPPORT COPPER supply lines at least every 6 feet with a plastic hanger. These hangers are easy to install (you slip them around the pipe, position them where you need them, then drive the nail they come with into a framing member). Because they're made of soft plastic, these hangers also help quiet noisy pipes and don't damage pipes during installation.

Before you solder existing plumbing

Dry the inside of pipes to create a tight joint. Stuff a piece of crustless white bread just upstream of the connection to absorb water. It dissolves later when the water is turned back on. Or insert a waxy capsule specially made to plug the line. When you're done soldering, apply heat where the capsule was lodged to melt it away.

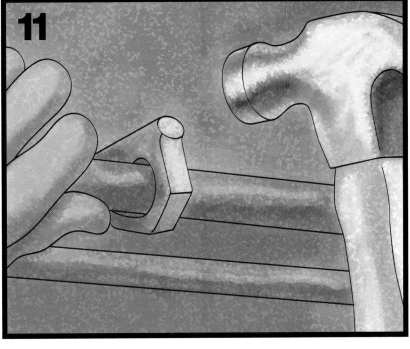

8

remodeling your basement

PREPARE TO SEE PAST THE DIM LIGHT, damp air, and crumbling floor of your current basement. Here, you'll find everything you need to know to transform the lowest floor of your home into a light, fresh, dry, cozy space that's ready to accept as fine a finish as any other room in your home. This chapter starts by taking a good look at your basement's present condition. Then it shows you how to test and repair damp, leaking, or uneven concrete walls or floors. To top it off you'll learn how to create new insulated surfaces and a below-ground entrance, which welcomes natural light into your new space. Let's get started!

A tucked-away bed In the basement can serve as guest quarters or a comfortably cool napping spot. The bunk *opposite* is a boxed-in twin mattress mounted to the wall on top of side-by-side chests. The interior is fitted with a wall-mounted reading lamp and a skinny wall shelf along the bed to hold a radio, books, and a glass of water. Thick curtains hung from a closet rod can be pulled shut for privacy.

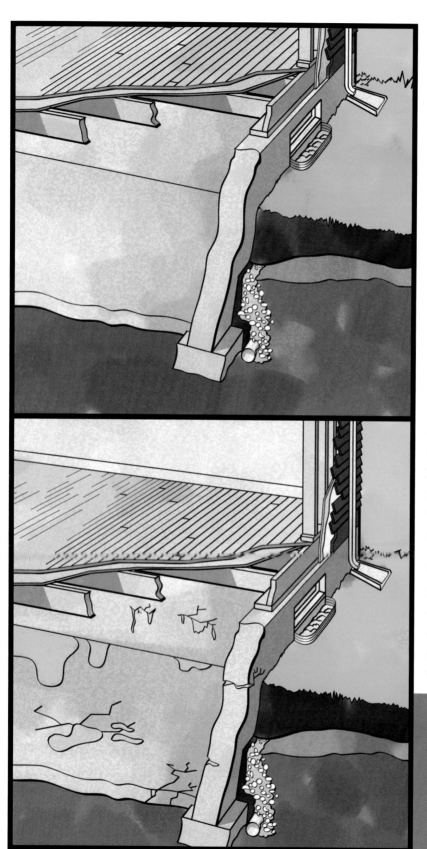

Find out why your basement is wet

Basements get damp—or downright swampy—for lots of reasons. Most causes are curable, although some require more effort and expense to eradicate than others. In any case take care of moisture problems before doing any remodeling work; then wait through a rainy season to make sure your basement stays dry. Left untreated, dampness causes mold, mildew, crumbling of the foundation, rot, deterioration, and rust. Wet walls or a wet floor, or worse, standing water, can reduce an otherwise fine basement renovation to a soggy mess in a single season.

Four types of moisture problems prevail. Condensation is relatively easy to deal with, but if you find seepage, leaks, or subterranean water, you'll need to make further repairs—then wait through another rainy period to ensure the problem is solved.

Condensation

SYMPTOMS AND TESTS Damp walls, dripping pipes, rusty hardware, and foul-smelling mildew are sometimes caused by condensation. Test by taping aluminum foil in the dampest

Cure dampness

Basements can get damp—or downright swampy—for lots of reasons. Left untreated dampness causes mold, mildew, and a crumbling foundation. Seal cracks, improve drainage, and deal with condensation before you start your remodeling job.

Test for condensation and seepage

Use duct tape to completely seal aluminum-foil squares to the floor and wall. Droplets forming on the undersides indicate that water is seeping in from the outside; droplets on top indicate condensation.

be poor drainage around the foundation or a leaky window.

SOLUTION Improve exterior drainage. If problems surface in the form of occasional minor damp spots, an interior sealer may work. But if the problem is widespread, persistent dampness, waterproof the outside of the foundation.

Leaks

SYMPTOMS AND TESTS
Localized wetness that seems to be oozing or even trickling from a wall or floor. It usually appears during heavy rain. Test by running a hose outside near the leak, then pay particular attention to mortar joints between blocks.

CAUSES Leaks typically appear around cracks that result from normal

spot. If the foil's face is foggy or beaded with water after 24 hours, suspect condensation.

CAUSES Excess humidity from an internal source, such as a basement shower, washing machine, or unvented dryer; or a significant difference between the wall temperature and inside air temperature.

SOLUTION Install a dehumidifier, improve ventilation by installing ventilating fans or opening windows during mild weather, and seal interior walls.

Seepage

SYMPTOMS AND TESTS
Dampness on a section of a wall or floor, most often on a wall near floor level, may be caused by seepage. Test as you do for condensation by taping aluminum foil to the wall. If moisture condenses on the back of the mirror after 24 hours, seepage is the culprit.

CAUSES Surface water forces its way through pores in the foundation or at an expansion joint where one slab of concrete joins another. The source may

Condensation

Condensation forms on cold-water pipes as well as on walls and floors. Using a dehumidifier helps, as does insulating the pipes. Two types of insulation are available: tape (top) and foam sleeve (bottom).

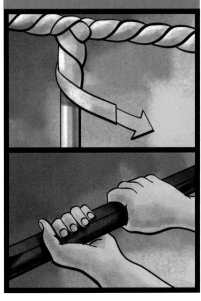

settling or improperly poured concrete. (If you see a cracklike line running horizontally across your basement wall, it may be that builders poured part of the wall and allowed it to harden before pouring the rest.) Faulty roof drainage or a grade that slopes toward the wall exacerbates the problem.

SOLUTION Improve exterior drainage. If the problem is localized to a few identifiable holes in the foundation wall, you may be able to simply plug those with hydraulic cement from the outside. If the problem is widespread leakage, waterproof the entire exterior of the foundation.

Subterranean water

SYMPTOMS AND TESTS A thin, barely noticeable film of water on the basement floor is often the first sign of this problem. Test by laying down plastic sheeting for two days. Check for penetrating moisture that dampens the concrete underneath.

CAUSES Usually a spring or a high water table forces water up from below under high pressure, turning your basement into a well. This may happen only during rainy periods.

SOLUTION Install a sump pump. Drainage tile around the perimeter of the foundation may help, but only if it drains to a low spot or a storm sewer.

Making and keeping your basement dry

When you know the cause of wetness, you can do what's needed to get rid of it. Start with the simplest solutions and move to more involved measures, as needed.

MAINTAIN YOUR GUTTERS AND DOWNSPOUTS Make sure they're clean, unobstructed, and in good condition with no leaks or blockages. Sometimes you can solve a problem by simply adding extensions to gutter downspouts or directing water away from the foundation.

CHECK YOUR GRADING Make sure the soil in your yard—and any concrete slabs, driveways, or patios—slopes away from the house. Test for slope by placing a smooth, round ball next to the foundation in several places: It should roll away from the foundation. If it doesn't, have the slab built up so it slopes away from the house. Soil around your foundation also should slope away. If not, bring in topsoil and regrade.

Brushing on interior sealer

You'll need:

- Brush with stiff bristles
- Cement-based sealer
- Mixing bucket
- Garden hose and adjustable spray nozzle

1 **CLEAN AWAY DIRT,** grease, and dust from the wall. (Sealers only work on bare concrete block or poured concrete, so if your wall has

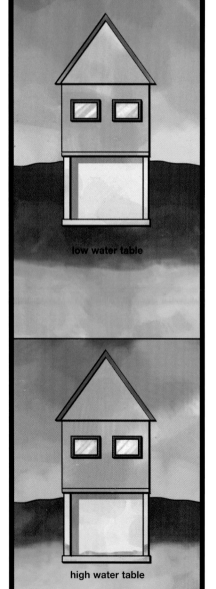

Water table

When the water table is low **top,** basements are dry. When the table is high **bottom,** such as after spring rains, moisture enters basements from several locations. A perimeter drain can help.

low water table

high water table

been previously painted, you're out of luck.) Thoroughly wet the wall with a fine mist from a garden hose. Thoroughly mix liquid and powder components of a cement-based sealer and apply with a stiff brush.

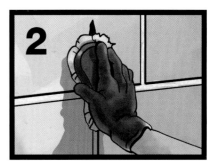

2 **AS YOU BRUSH,** fill in all the pores in the wall. Go over cracks several times, if necessary, to fill them. If a crack is too large to fill with sealer, fill it first with hydraulic cement. Some sealers have to stay wet for several days to ensure bonding. Apply a second coat, if necessary.

Sealing cracks from the inside with hydraulic cement

You'll need:

- Hammer
- Cold chisel
- Shop vacuum
- Mixing bucket

1 **USE A COLD CHISEL** (named for its ability to cut cold metal) to chisel minor cracks and holes so that they are wider at the bottom than they are at the top. This helps prevent the patch from popping out after it

---

Install a drainage system

To install an interior-perimeter drainage system *top*, you can remove the perimeter of the basement slab, dig a trench, fill it with gravel and a drainpipe that leads to a sump pump, then repair the slab. A less-invasive option is to glue a hollow plastic molding to the wall *bottom* that will trap water and channel it to a sump pump for removal.

Top illustration labels: drainage gap · slab broken out then repaired · existing slab · footing

Bottom illustration labels: hollow plastic base molding · existing slab · footing

sets. Make the hole at least ½ inch deep. Then vacuum out any dust and concrete fragments.

2 MIX CEMENT IN A BUCKET, adding water to dry mix until it has a puttylike consistency. Then work it by hand. When plugging a hole, roll it into the shape of a plug. For a crack, roll a long, snakelike shape.

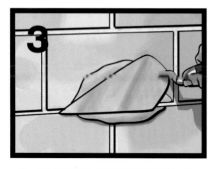

3 SQUEEZE THE MATERIAL into the opening. Keep working and applying pressure to the patch to make sure it fills every tiny crevice. Most cements will set even if water is leaking through the hole at the time of the repair (in which case the water should stop running). Apply pressure to the patch for several minutes to allow it to set.

joist

brackets

discharge pipe

basket

pump

Sump pumps

A sump pump pumps water out of a sump—a hole beneath the basement floor—so the basement itself doesn't flood. Combined with tight walls and floors and a dehumidifier, it keeps your basement pleasantly dry.

Installing a sump pump

You'll need:

- Sledge or rented jackhammer
- Gravel
- Concrete mix
- Mixing container
- Trowel
- Sump-pump kit
- ¾-inch plywood
- Drill

1 BREAK A HOLE in the floor slab. Make it about 6 inches wider and 4 inches deeper than the pump basket. Use a rented jackhammer or sledge. Put 4 inches of gravel in the hole, insert the basket, and backfill the sides. Trowel concrete level with the basket.

2 LOWER THE PUMP into the basket and connect the drain line to the discharge line. Make electrical connections, as required (some models simply plug into a nearby outlet).

3 MAKE A COVER, if necessary. Drill holes for pipes and wire through ¾-inch plywood. Then saw the board in half—cutting through the center of the holes—to install the cover.

Sealing a wall from the outside

You'll need:

- Shovel
- Broom with stiff bristles
- Hose
- Mortar and trowel (optional)
- Brushes and/or rollers to apply sealer
- Drainpipe
- Heavy-gauge polyethylene sheeting
- Perforated drainpipe

1 EXCAVATE TO THE problem area. If the problem is fairly high up on the foundation wall, you may be able to do the digging yourself with a shovel. Otherwise hire a contractor to dig a trench wide enough for you to work in. Remove dirt that's close to the wall by hand, and brush the wall clean.

2 APPLY SEALER. You can hire contractors who specialize in this application, or you can do it yourself. Wash the wall clean, allow it to dry, and apply two coats of tarlike bituminous sealer. Or back-plaster the wall with two coats of mortar; then apply the sealer.

3 INSTALL PERFORATED DRAINPIPE and a polyethylene barrier. Dig a trench along the footing and install a sloping, perforated drainpipe embedded in gravel. Stick heavy-gauge polyethylene sheeting to the wall sealer. Drape it over the footing but not the gravel drain. Overlap all seams by least 6 inches.

Basement floors

After you solve moisture problems, your main concern becomes the basement floor: Is it sound and level enough to finish with your floor covering choice? If your floor shows no signs of moisture problems, is level (no high spots of more than ⅛ inch in 10 feet), and is not severely cracked, it may need only surface repairs before you install underlayment (in areas you intend to cover with vinyl) or a finished floor. If it's badly cracked, broken, or damaged, you'll have to resurface it, either with self-leveling compound or new cement.

Surface repairs

You'll need:

- 6-foot carpenter's level
- Marking pencil
- Patching compound
- Trowel
- Rented concrete grinder
- Hydraulic cement
- Muriatic acid
- Mop

First check the floor's surface for evenness by rotating a 6-foot level on the floor in sections. Mark dips or high spots with a carpenter's pencil. Repair those areas as follows:

Dewatering devices

DEHUMIDIFIERS are rated by how much they can dehumidify and how many pints of water per hour they can remove from the air. Know the square footage of your basement before you buy, and make sure you purchase an appliance that has enough capacity to do the job. Most units are automatic and can be set either to run continuously or maintain a preset humidity level—a convenient feature. The units have removable basins or buckets to catch the water—most with a knockout at the bottom where you can attach a tube or hose that you can run directly into a floor drain. Otherwise you need to remember to empty the machine periodically. Dehumidifiers remove moisture from the air that can cause condensation, mold, and mildew. They work best if the source of moisture comes from within the house—from using a bath or shower or washing clothes, for example—and do nothing to prevent water from entering the room. They also add heat to the space they dehumidify so, in warm climates, consider dehumidifying a basement with an air-conditioner instead.

SUMP PUMPS are rated according to how many gallons of water per minute they can pump and how high they can lift the water. Battery-powered sump pumps work during short power outages—useful if short, violent storms often cause your basement's flooding. Most sump pumps exhaust water through a plastic pipe buried in a shallow trench in your yard and carry the water to a street gutter where it flows into a storm drain or to a distant low spot on your property. Connecting a sump pump to a sewer line is not recommended: It can overload the sewer line, especially in homes with septic systems.

LOWS AND HIGHS Fill depressions with patching compound, troweling them smooth and feathering them to the surrounding floor. Rent a concrete grinder to level high spots. Check the surface of your repairs with a straight-edge, continuing to fill or grind until the floor is flat and level.

CRACKS AND HOLES Use hydraulic cement to repair, as described on pages 143–144.

SALT DEPOSITS White or yellow alkaline deposits impair adhesive bonding on glued-down floor coverings. To remove them mop the floor with a solution of four parts water and one part muriatic acid; then rinse the slab with clean water. Muriatic acid is extremely caustic, so follow package directions carefully.

Resurfacing

You'll need

FOR SELF-LEVELING

- Self-leveling primer and compound
- Brush or roller
- Mixing bucket
- Floor squeegee
- Aggregate (optional, depending on required thickness of the compound)

FOR POURING A NEW SLAB

- 6-mil polyethylene sheeting
- ½-inch rigid foam sheeting
- 6×6-inch #10 wire mesh
- Bricks or blocks

If your floor is extensively damaged and can't be repaired using the preceding techniques—or, if such repairs would be too time-consuming—you still have two more good options for making a lasting repair. Before you choose either, though, consult a structural engineer to determine the cause of your floor's damage and to ensure that its condition is stable enough that further damage won't likely follow.

SELF-LEVELING COMPOUND is a liquid mortar that you pour and spread onto a sloped, rough, uneven, but structurally sound, floor. Most compounds require that you first coat the floor with a primer. After the primer has cured, you mix the compound and spread it onto the floor—up to ½ inch thick—with a floor squeegee. The compound levels itself and dries hard and smooth. If you need a thickness greater than ½ inch, add aggregate to the mix.

A NEW SLAB If your floor is not structurally sound, you don't have to break up the old slab and start again. You can pour a new slab right over the old one as long as the increase in floor height leaves you enough headroom (consult your local building codes for minimum ceiling height requirements). First install any new plumbing. Then lay a waterproof membrane, such as 6-mil polyethylene plastic sheeting, over the old slab as a moisture barrier, overlapping edges by at least 4 inches. Then lay ½-inch rigid foam around the perimeter of the floor as an expansion barrier, and suspend 6×6-inch #10 wire mesh on brick or pieces of block to center the wire in the concrete when it is poured. Pour at least 4 inches of concrete and finish it with a float.

Installing a branch drain

You'll need:

- Chalk line
- Circular saw with masonry blade
- Sledge or rented jackhammer
- Shovel
- Tape measure
- Chain cutter, reciprocating saw, or hacksaw
- Pipe and fittings
- Torpedo level

If you want a new bathroom in the basement and you can't piggyback the new drain lines to the old, you may have to tie into the old lines with a new branch line. This means breaking up the concrete and installing new lines and fittings. It's heavy work, but it's not technically difficult. Before you tear into the floor, make sure you know exactly where the existing lines run.

1 MARK POSITION of existing drain and branch line on floor with chalk lines. Have new fixtures (shower, toilet, sink) on hand before you map drain lines; plumbing locations need to be precise.

2 SCORE LINES using a circular saw fitted with a masonry blade.

Then break up concrete between lines with a sledge or a rented electric jackhammer. After you remove the first chunk, dig out the dirt under the remaining sections as far as you can—concrete is easier to break if there's no soil beneath it.

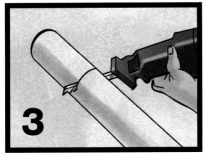

3 IF YOU AREN'T SURE of the nominal size of the existing line, measure it so you will know what size fitting to buy. Mark the position of the new fitting carefully on the old line. Cut the line with a chain cutter, reciprocating saw, or hacksaw.

4 INSTALL A NO-HUB FITTING on either side of the cut line.

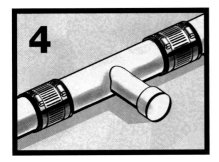

Adjust it with a torpedo level to ensure the correct fall (or slope), then tighten the no-hub clamps.

5 INSTALL THE new drain line (see page 132 for details).

6 RE-CHECK the fall of the line over its length and adjust it at either end, if necessary. Pour and finish new concrete.

Installing a wood subfloor

You'll need:

- Shop vacuum
- Detergent
- Garage brush
- Bucket
- Hose
- Fan or dehumidifier
- Asphalt primer
- Brush
- Asphalt mastic
- Trowel
- 15-lb. felt paper or 6-mil polyurethelene sheeting
- Chalk line
- Pressure-treated 2×4s
- Mason's line
- 8d masonry nails, powder-actuated fasteners, or concrete screws
- Hammer drill and masonry bit (if using concrete screws)
- 1½-inch polystyrene insulation
- Construction adhesive
- ⅝- or ¾-inch underlayment-rated plywood
- Ringshank underlayment nails

A wood subfloor with sleepers (floor joists that rest directly on the concrete floor) solves a variety of basement flooring problems. Use sleepers to protect a floor from condensation or as an alternative to a liquid leveler when you don't want to fix cracks, tilts, or imperfections. You can also install sleepers if you want to insulate the floor. You must install a wood subfloor if your finished floor is the kind that has to be nailed down.

Although a wood subfloor covers minor cracks and imperfections, its installation begins with a thorough cleaning of the concrete floor. Vacuum the floor, then clean it with a detergent solution and garage brush. Rinse it, and let it dry.

1 SEAL THE SURFACE with an asphalt primer. When the primer has cured, trowel the slab with asphalt mastic to a depth of about ⅛ inch. Don't trowel yourself into a corner; work toward the doorway.

2 STARTING AT THE DOOR unroll 15-pound felt paper or 6-mil polyethylene sheets onto the mastic, pressing them into the surface to

Install a finished wall

Cover the masonry walls in your basement with a moisture barrier, studding, insulation, and eventually wallboard and paint, and you'll have a room that's as snug, dry, warm, and attractive as those on your home's main floors.

remove air bubbles and overlapping successive sheets by 6 inches.

3 SNAP CHALK LINES on the moisture barrier at 16-inch intervals. Leaving a ½-inch gap at the wall and at the ends of the sleepers, center pressure-treated 2×4s on the chalk lines. Stretch a mason's line tightly across the surface to make

sure sleepers are level; shim those that aren't.

4 FASTEN A SLEEPER to the concrete with 8d masonry nails, powder-actuated fasteners, or concrete screws. To use screws drill a pilot hole through the sleeper to mark the moisture barrier. Lay the sleeper aside, drill concrete with a masonry

bit and hammer drill, and install screws in sleepers with a power screwdriver.

5 IF YOU WANT TO insulate the floor, cut pieces of 1½-inch polystyrene insulation to fit between sleepers.

6 LAY A HEAD of construction adhesive on top of sleepers, and nail ⅝- or ¾-inch underlayment-rated plywood over them, staggering joints and leaving ⅛-inch gaps between them, ½-inch gaps at walls.

Insulating basement walls

Boost your basement's energy efficiency and save on heating and cooling cost by insulating the outside walls. Rigid foam panels do the job best. Foam offers more insulating value than fiberglass batts and in less space. Foam is also ideal when paired with masonry; it's impervious to moisture and water, and can be covered with drywall without studs.

The best way to install foam board is with steel Z-channels. These eliminate the need for glue and allow for a continuous insulation, unbroken by studs or furring strips (studs and strips act as a thermal bridge, reducing insulation efficiency).

Installing rigid foam insulation with Z-channels

You'll need:

- ■ Z-channels
- ■ Powder-actuated fasteners
- ■ Rigid foam insulation
- ■ Carpenter's level
- ■ Tape measure
- ■ Marking pencil
- ■ Serrated knife

Install a piece of Z-channel in one corner with the wall flange pointing into the corner. Leave enough room to slip in a piece of foam and a piece of drywall along the adjacent wall. Attach the channel with powder-actuated fasteners. Use a #3 load with a ½ inch pin, five per channel.

Cut rigid foam with a serrated kitchen knife. Slip a piece of foam under the Z-channel. Trap it in place with a second piece of channel. The wall flange should point in the opposite direction. Continue in this manner until you reach the next corner. The channels have a slight angle built into

them, allowing them to grip the insulation as it is installed.

Cut the last piece of foam so the final Z-channel fits into the corner with enough room for a piece of foam and a piece of drywall on the adjacent wall. Start adjacent walls by slipping insulation into the gap you left.

Installing basement doors and windows

A new window or door installed in an exterior basement wall brings in lots of air and natural light. But creating necessary wall openings is a major project. If you do this project on your own, consult with a structural engineer, architect, or building contractor on how to proceed.

First you'll install a header or lintel in the opening's top to bear the weight of the house. You'll need to make holes in your basement walls for the doors and windows. If they're made of a solid slab of reinforced concrete, this isn't a job for a do-it-yourselfer. Hire a firm that specializes in concrete sawing. You can, however, cut through a block wall with a rented rotary hammer and cold chisels.

To install a below-grade door or a window with a sill that falls below grade, you have to excavate a window well to keep soil and rainfall way from its exterior surface. You probably can do much of the excavating in connection with breaching the wall (described below). An above-grade door doesn't require a well, but you must keep soil at least 6 inches away from the bottom sill.

Digging the well

You'll need:

- ■ Shovel
- ■ Wheelbarrow

Break through and remove sod around the location of a new door or window. (Keep soil for backfilling the well liner; use sod to fill any bare spots in your lawn. Add unused soil to gardens.)

Excavate to a depth that accommodates the drainage system you plan to use: about 2 feet lower than the sill for an independent drain line that leads to a lower section of your property. Dig to the foundation if you plan to tie the well drain to an existing perimeter system on the exterior. To construct a light well for your window or small patio outside a below-grade doorway, excavate to dimensions that accommodate your design (see page 152). Consider hiring a backhoe operator to dig your drain-line trench if the trench runs deep and across a large expanse of lawn. You don't need to be exact with the excavation for the well itself. Allow plenty of elbowroom when you cut and frame the opening; you can backfill it later.

Breaching the wall

You'll need:

- ■ Circular saw with both wood and masonry blades
- ■ Tape measure
- ■ Marking pencil
- ■ Speed square

- 2×4s
- Nails
- Hammer
- Small sledgehammer
- Cold chisel

1 ERECT A TEMPORARY support wall framed with 2×6 lumber about 4 feet inside the exterior wall you want to breach and longer than the wall opening you want to create. Remove any existing windows. Locate the new opening using a section drawing.

2 MARK CUTTING LINES for a rough opening on wall's interior and exterior surfaces. Mark an opening large enough to accommodate wood framing for the unit you're installing. Make the wall breach 3 inches wider to accommodate 2×4 framing on both sides, and higher than the rough opening specified by they unit's manufacturer. Score cut lines with a circular saw fitted with a masonry blade. Make several passes, ¼ inch deeper each time, on both sides of the wall. Then score another line down the vertical center of the opening so you can easily remove blocks.

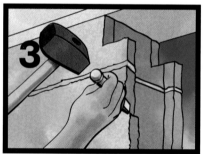

3 TAP OUT BLOCKS with a small sledgehammer. Start at scored center line and work toward edges. Finish edges flush, as shown above.

Framing and installing

You'll need:

- Pressure-treated lumber
- Circular saw
- Tape measure and marking pencil
- Speed square
- Galvanized deck screws
- Concrete mix
- Mixing bucket
- Trowel
- Polyurethane caulk
- Trim stock
- Paint

1 USE PRESSURE-TREATED lumber for all framing members used for an exterior wall. The size of the framing—window bucks for a window and king and jack studs for a door—depends on the thickness of the window unit. Header stock is sized for the unit's dimensions and for the weight the header will carry. Measure and cut header stock and assemble the pieces.

2 INSTALL FRAMING, header first, then top and bottom framing, then side members or jack and king studs. Fasten framing to the concrete block with galvanized deck screws (if block will hold the screws), toggle bolts, or other masonry fasteners. Till bottom buck slightly to outside to shed rainwater. Seal gaps between framing and block with concrete. When concrete has cured fill any remaining gaps around edges outside and inside with polyurethane caulk.

3 INSTALL WINDOWS by fastening window casing to bucks with galvanized deck screws; install cladding if window has aluminum-clad casings. Install the unit using the techniques in the illustrations, above. Trim or finish exterior to prevent erosion from damaging your work.

Trimming the interior

You'll need:

- 1× lumber
- Nails
- Furring strips
- Rigid foam insulation
- Drywall
- Hammer
- Nails
- Tape measure
- Marking pencil
- Circular saw
- Speed square

Basement windows present some unique trim challenges. Thick basement walls tend to make windows seem small, and a window's height may interfere with a suspended ceiling. Tackle these challenges by beveling edges of wall and trim around the window to reveal more of the window area.

Fasten beveled 1× stock along the perimeter of the window frame at an angle between 10 and 30 degrees.

Bevel horizontal furring strips or the tops of studs in a stud wall. Fasten 1× blocking between studs to provide a surface for nailing the drywall.

Insulate with rigid foam insulation and finish with drywall.

Attach a 1× nailer at the window's top frame; angle the edge panels of a suspended ceiling from ceiling hangers to nailer.

Installing a window-well liner

You'll need:

- Prefabricated fiberglass or steel window-well liners
- Electric drill or hammer drill
- Masonry anchors
- Screws
- Gravel
- Shovel
- Wheelbarrow
- Ladder (if required by code)
- Soil tamper

Prefabricated fiberglass or steel window liners aren't heavy but positioning and attaching them requires a helper. Before installing a liner complete the excavation and installation of any drain lines that the well may need (see page 132.)

Hold the liner in place against the outside wall so its top edge sits 4 to 6 inches above the soil line.

Mark the wall for the position of fasteners. Drill holes for masonry anchors and fasten liner to wall with them.

Fill the well bottom with gravel until it's level with the drain cover. Then backfill the outside of the liner, tamping as you go.

Install a ladder if your local codes require one. (Most local codes will require a ladder for window wells deeper than 44 inches.)

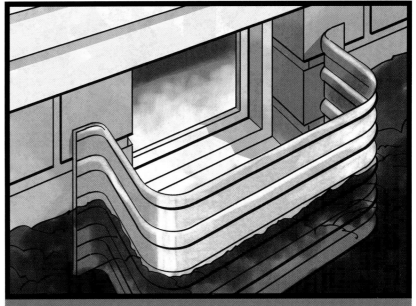

Window-well liner

Window well-liners hold back the soil, allowing you to install a window below ground level for additional natural light and ventilation. Although digging the hole requires some muscle, the liners themselves are not difficult to install.

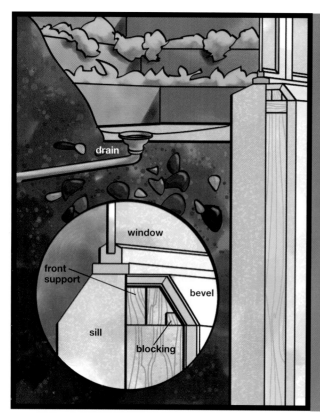

drain

window

front support

bevel

sill

blocking

Below-grade windows and doors

A terraced window well *left* is a great way to welcome sunshine and views into a subterranean space. Dig the well in a funnel shape, stairstepping the sides and holding back the dirt with retaining walls of treated landscape timbers or masonry landscaping blocks. Install a drain at the well's bottom to handle water runoff. Plant the horizontal surfaces with flowers or low-maintenance greenery for a restful view. To make sure as much light as possible penetrates to the room, you can bevel the ceiling up, if necessary, so it does not obstruct the top of the window. You can bevel the sides and bottom of the window casing as well.

A below-grade entrance *opposite* can be a great addition to your basement. It allows entrance directly from the outdoors, without having to make your way through the house. Consider installing one early in your remodeling project to minimize dirt, disruption, and damage to the walls and floors of your main living area as you bring materials and supplies to your job site. Either dig the well yourself or hire an excavating contractor to do it. Waterproof the exterior walls of the well and install a perimeter drain before backfilling. Use steel stringers and weatherproof treads for the stairway; wood may rot.

Installing a below-grade entrance

You'll need:

- Steel stringers
- Stairsteps made for outdoor use
- Shovel
- Tape measure
- Drain pipe
- Rebar
- Concrete
- Concrete block
- Mortar
- Carpenter's level
- Mason's line
- Nails
- Hatch door or prefabricated green house enclosure

A below-grade entrance enhances any basement and provides years of added convenience. First order a prefabricated steel stringer and steps made for outdoor use. Then excavate an area large enough for retaining walls and stairs. Dig 4 inches below the foundation's bottom, building the area as large as you can. Excavate trenches for wall footings to dimensions required by your local code.

Set horizontal lengths of rebar in the trench and pour footings. Push vertical rebar into the center of the wet concrete in the trench every 24 inches. Let the concrete cure.

Install a perimeter drain around the area; tie it into an existing drainage system or direct runoff to a lower area of your yard.

Enclose the area with cement-block retaining walls to a height that's even with or slightly above grade. Start laying block at the corners.

Waterproof the wall exterior with asphalt emulsion or use some other method required by code.

Breach the basement wall and install a door using techniques outlined on pages 149–150.

Build stairs. Install steel stringers and steps according to the manufacturer's specifications.

For a finished look cover the area with a hatch door or shelter to create a weathertight entrance. A prefabricated greenhouse makes an attractive entry and brings in extra light. Either choice requires a poured concrete cap on top of the retaining walls.

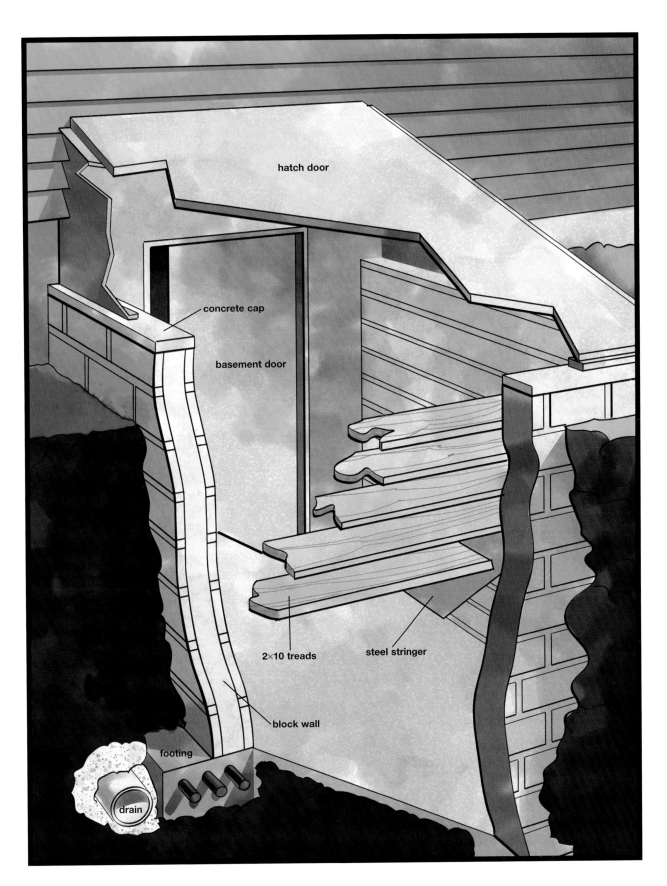

hatch door

concrete cap

basement door

2×10 treads

steel stringer

block wall

footing

drain

9

remodeling your attic

THE BENEFIT OF WORKING IN MOST ATTICS AND BONUS ROOMS is that

you get to start with a pretty clean slate: Attics often are unfinished, making them

very agreeable to running utilities, building walls, and installing windows, dormers, and

other structural modifications. Because you're dealing with a sloped roof rather than

the relatively square box that makes up most basements, you'll expand your carpentry

skills by doing projects, such as framing in dormers and building partition and knee

walls. None of it is beyond the scope of a patient, well-equipped do-it-yourselfer,

though, so let's get going!

A daybed fits perfectly beneath the pitched roof of this attic guest area *opposite*. A glossy red-and-black-painted floor border pulls the focus to the floor; it's a snappy contrast to the textural, whitewashed floor- and wallboards. The closet door behind the bed was purposefully styled with a rustic look; there's nothing essential behind it.

installing attic stairs

The job of constructing a stairway begins with a hole in the attic floor; one that's already there or one you cut. Whether you're enlarging existing stairs or building a new stairway, the procedure is essentially the same. You can orient your stairwell opening either perpendicular to or parallel with the attic floor joists. Parallel construction requires less cutting.

Marking and cutting an opening

1 ERECT TEMPORARY SUPPORTS perpendicular to the attic floor joists and about 2 feet beyond your proposed stair location.

2 LAY OUT the perimeter of the opening on the attic floor or on the floor joists using your detailed floor plan as a guide. Snap chalk lines to mark where you will make cuts—at the finished width of your stairwell.

3 CUT ALONG the chalk lines using a circular saw with a carbide tipped blade set to the depth of any existing flooring.

4 REMOVE ANY FLOORING and insulation.

5 DISCONNECT AND RE-ROUTE plumbing and wiring (see pages 126–137).

6 AT THE CORNERS DRILL HOLES through the ceiling below. Snap chalk lines between the holes in the ceiling material and cut it away. If you're not removing the entire ceiling, use techniques for removing wallboard or plaster on page 119.

7 USE A SQUARE to extend the perimeter line of the opening down the face of any joists to be cut. Have a helper support the joists or support them with temporary 2×4s as you cut them with a reciprocating saw.

8 CUT TRIMMER joists and header stock to the dimensions of the opening and nail them with 16d nails staggered at 12-inch intervals.

9 FRAME THE WALLS for an enclosed stairwell.

Hanging the stairs

1 MARK AND CUT the stringer, fasten it to the new headers and to the floor below, and install the risers and treads.

2 POSTPONE INSTALLING the handrail until the finishing stage of your project. It will be in the way as you move tools and materials into the attic during construction.

New attic floors and ceilings

Making changes to attic floors and ceilings involves special techniques. For

---

Installing attic stairs

You can use one of two methods for installing attic stairs, depending upon whether the stairs will run parallel with the joists *left* or perpendicular to the joists *right*. The latter requires much more cutting and the building of a temporary support wall.

PARALLEL   PERPENDICULAR

temporary support wall   temporary support wall

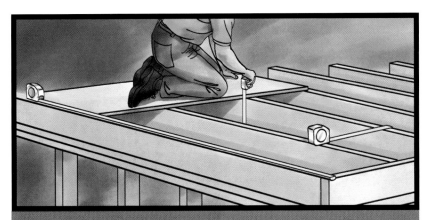

Measuring joist size, spacing, and span

Measure size from bottom of joist to top edge, spacing from the far edge of one joist to the near edge of the next, and span from inside edges of cap plate.

example, new joists have to span the attic floor completely—from the outer edges of one top plate to the other—or join above bearing walls. In almost all cases you have to angle the top corner of the new joists to fit snugly against the roof sheathing.

Adding new joists means working across the unfinished surface of the old joists. To work comfortably and avoid stepping through the ceiling below, lay temporary catwalks of either 2-inch stock or loose plywood sheets across the old joists. After you cut the joist angles, lay the new joists in their locations without fastening them so you minimize the time spent walking on your temporary flooring.

Cutting corners

1 **TO MEASURE** the angle for the joist ends, get as close as you can to the top plate and slide the base of a T-bevel gauge along the top of an existing joist. Adjust the blade of the gauge so it lies against the bottom of the rafter.

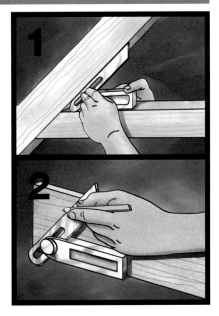

2 **TIGHTEN THE BEVEL** and transfer the angle to a new joist. Repeat for the other end of the joist. After determining the correct angle, cut all the joists at the same time.

3 **TOENAIL** new joists into place.

Adding new joists

You have two options when adding new joists to an attic floor. Which you

choose depends on the size of the existing framing stock. In either case, if your plans include a partition wall, double the joists under the wall and leave a 3-inch space between them for wiring or plumbing. Fastening new joists may be difficult—the angle of the rafters at the eaves may not leave you enough room to swing a hammer, which can also damage ceilings below. Use a nail gun or drive screws.

IF YOUR EXISTING JOISTS are 2×4 stock, install an independent set of new joists between the old ones. Space the new joists evenly and support them on 2×4 blocks so they clear the existing wiring. Or drill the new stock and re-thread the wires. Toenail the new joists to the cap plates with three 16d nails at each end. If you have to lap them over a long span, center the joint on the cap plate of a lower load-bearing wall. Either face-nail the overlapped sides of the joint or reinforce butt-joined ends with a 2-foot length of plywood on each side. Secure the joint with 16d nails and toenail it to the top plate of the supporting wall.

IF YOUR EXISTING JOISTS are 2×8 or larger, attach a new set to the old. Your building codes may require bridging, usually every 10 running feet over bearing walls. Start by clamping the joists together and toenailing the new joists to the cap plates with 16d nails. Leave clamps in place and stagger 16d nails at 12-inch intervals along the joist. Replace bridging as you go.

Laying an attic subflooor

Using the tools, techniques, and materials described on page 156, install plywood subfloor over your floor joists. Begin along the eaves or on a centerline marked on the joists with chalk. Stagger the joints. There is no structural need for heavier plywood in areas used only for storage—½-inch material is ample for storage weight. It isn't necessary to lay flooring behind knee walls if the area won't be used; however, laying a floor over unused space keeps dust and

Getting joists to the attic

If your attic conversion requires strengthening the floor by adding joists, getting the new joist lumber up to the attic may be your most difficult task. The joists required to span your attic floor may be too long to make the turns up the stairs.

If you're planning a new stairwell, bring up the joists through the opening before you hang the stringers. The rough opening should provide enough room.

If that doesn't work consider stripping away a long section of roofing at the eaves and sliding the joists in from the roof or from scaffolding outside the house. Using outside access also makes it easier to trim the top corners of the joists to fit the rafter angle where the joists butt against the roofing sheathing.

insulation fibers from migrating into living areas.

Installing ceiling joists

Aside from the nooks and crannies associated with attic construction, finished attics usually have either cathedral or flat ceilings.

CATHEDRAL CEILING If you opt for a cathedral ceiling, your rafters are your framing. You can leave the collar ties in place as long as they're spaced 4 feet on center; raise them one at a time or replace them with knee walls where codes permit.

FLAT CEILING Unless the collar ties are at the correct height and meet code for the ceiling span, a flat ceiling requires the addition of ceiling joists (usually 2×4s or 2×6s). Use the same procedures for determining the ceiling joist angle as you do for floor joists, and

face-nail them to the rafters. Drive one 16d nail at one end, level the joist, and fasten the other end. Then finish nailing both ends.

Building a shed dormer

Crafting a shed dormer calls for basic carpentry skills and experience with rafters. If you don't have the skills, you can hire a carpenter to cut through the existing roof and frame the dormer for you. The front wall can either be placed flush with the exterior of the house or set back. A set-back design is more appealing, but it requires the attic floor joists to support the dormer wall. Before you start a set-back dormer, strengthen the floor by adding joists and lay a subfloor to support the framing.

Finding the slope

Draw a section plan for your dormer. Include the following:

MAIN-ROOF SLOPE is the distance a surface rises along a horizontal length. The slope of your main roof is a ratio of its height (attic floor to peak) to the distance from eave to the peak. In the example *opposite top,* the pitch is 8 in 12—the roof rises 8 inches for every horizontal foot. To determine the slope of your roof, use a level and a framing square, as shown in the illustration. The place where the rafter intersects the square is its rise per foot.

DORMER PLACEMENT Draw an accurate profile of your dormer and experiment with placement of the front wall and roof pitch. Aside from the

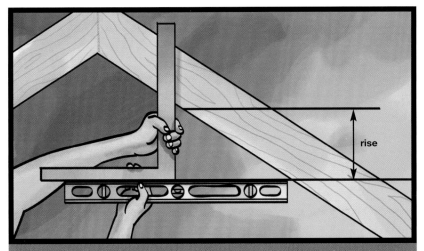

Finding the slope

The first step in building any type of dormer is to find the slope of the roof, or the distance that it rises along a horizontal length, using a level and framing square.

it from the opposite side of the rafter. Repeat this process for all of the remaining header sections.

5 REMOVE THE TEMPORARY walls and frame the front wall with the top plate extended 3½ inches (for the corner posts) on both end studs.

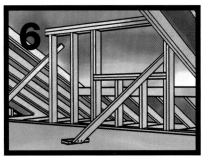

6 SET THE WALL up and brace it. Face-nail the sill plate to the floor, toenail the studs to the rafter header, and face-nail the end studs to the rafters.

pitch required by code, dormer configuration is largely a matter of aesthetics.

Building the dormer

1 CREATE A LAYOUT. Snap chalk lines on your attic floor directly below the dormer opening. Drop a plumb bob from the rafters down to the corners of the chalk lines and mark the rafters. Reinforce the two rafters at the edges of the opening and drive nails through the roof at the marks.

2 SNAP CHALK LINES between the nails on the outside of the

roof and then strip off the roofing 12 inches beyond the lines. Snap the lines onto the sheathing. With a circular saw set to the depth of the sheathing, cut the sheathing and remove it.

3 MARK THE RAFTERS and erect your temporary walls just beyond the marks (see page 124 for instructions on building a wall in place). Cut the rafters at the marks.

4 INSTALL DOUBLE HEADERS. Nail double 2×8 joist hangers to the reinforced rafters at each of the corners of the opening. Slide one header into the hanger and nail

7 BUILD THE CORNER POSTS from doubled 2×4s and 5-inch plywood scraps. Cut their bottom ends to the angle of slope of the roof. Face-nail the posts to the end studs and top plate and toenail them to the rafters under the sheathing.

8 CUT THE RAFTERS by setting a framing square on one rafter so the measurements of the dormer-roof slope intersect it, as shown.

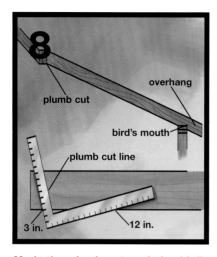

Mark the plumb cut and the bird's mouth (the v-shape cutout that defines where the rafter is nailed to the top); then test-fit the rafter and make any adjustments. Use this rafter as a template to cut the others.

9 MARK THE HEADER and the top plate for the rafters, and hang them on the header with sloping rafter hangers. Toenail the rafters to the front-wall top plate. Frame and sheath the end walls; finish the dormer with roofing, siding, and windows.

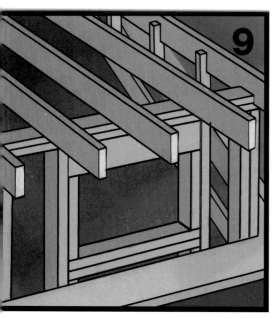

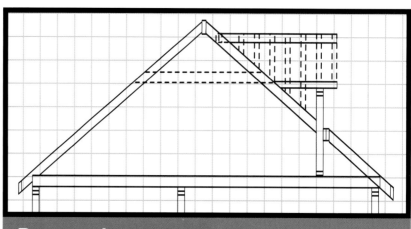

Draw a plan

Draw your dormer out carefully on graph paper before you start building to make sure it will look just right.

Building a gable dormer

A gable dormer is a small room with a peaked roof built perpendicular to the main roofline.

Constructing a gable dormer is a bit more complicated than constructing a shed dormer. The top plates of the sidewalls are level, and a ridge board between them supports the roof peak and pairs of rafters. Still, the construction of a gable dormer proceeds in the same order as a shed dormer. Before you start, strengthen the floor with additional joists to support the dormer framing.

Finding a slope

Before you begin construction draw a section (or profile) view of it. Using the same techniques used for a shed dormer on page 158, find the pitch of your existing roof and draw it to scale on graph paper.

Then draw in the sidewalls to scale and determine the pitch of the dormer

roof. The pitch is the amount of rise in inches (measured from the top plate of the dormer sidewall) for every horizontal foot, from the edge of the wall to the centerline of the roof peak. The dormer ridge line is horizontal. In the example the rise is 6 in 12, but the pitch of your particular dormer roof will depend on the look of the dormer itself and the pitch of the main roof. Make sketches on tracing paper to get

Cutting compound miters

The valley rafters and the common and jack rafters that fit against them are cut with compound miters. The angle of the cut conforms to both the downward slope of the boards and the angle where it is attached. To cut a compound miter:
MARK THE RAFTER at its longest length from the end of one angle to the farthest end on the other side.
DUPLICATE THE ANGLE of downward slope with an angle gauge and mark it on the rafter.
SET YOUR CIRCULAR SAW at a 45-degree bevel and cut along the lines.

the design right. Then draw the dormer on your final section plan.

Cutting and framing

With your section plan as a guide, follow the techniques for building a shed dormer to lay out the gable dormer and cut the opening.

1 LAY OUT dormer location on the attic floor and transfer the outline to the rafters with a plumb bob.

2 MARK THE ROOF exterior at the corners and cut the opening through the roof.

3 BUILD temporary support walls, mark and cut the rafters, and reinforce the rafters at the edge of the opening. Install double headers at the top and bottom of the opening.

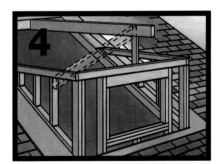

4 FRAME THE FRONT wall and the sidewalls with a doubled top plate as shown, overlapping the front-wall cap plates on the sidewalls and extending the tops of the sidewalls 13½ inches past the front wall. This supports the rake rafters.

Installing the ridge

The ridge is supported at the top by the header and at the bottom by a 2×4

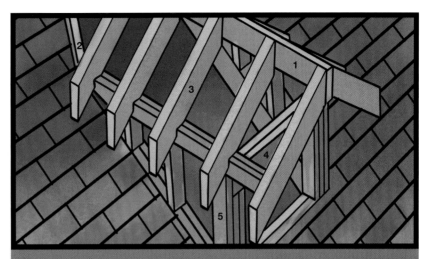

Components of a gable dormer

Gable dormers have five framing components: 1) the ridge, 2) the valley rafters, 3) common rafters, 4) double header, and 5) studs.

ridge stud fastened to the front-wall top plate.

Cut the ridge to length (the length of the sidewalls, plus the front-wall framing thickness, plus 1 foot overhang).

Assemble the ridge and ridge stud. The length of the ridge stud equals the rise of the dormer roof minus the width of the ridge board. In the example it's 18½ inches (24 inches minus 5½ inches, the 2×6 width).

Cut the ridge stud and toenail it 12 inches from the outer end of the ridge board. Lift the assembly into place and fasten the top end to the header in a joist hanger. Toenail the ridge stud to the top plate of the front wall with 10d nails. Level the ridge. Mark the ridge and top plates at 16-inch intervals.

Cutting rafters

Four kinds of rafters make up a gable dormer; each type requires different cuts. Label them as you cut them.

RAKE RAFTERS are the two front

rafters and form the overhang.

COMMON RAFTERS run from the front wall to the valley.

VALLEY RAFTERS run from the intersection of the ridge and header to the sidewalls.

JACK RAFTERS are the short rafters that run from the ridge and header to the valley rafters.

1 LAY YOUR framing square on one end of a common rafter with the pitch measurements intersecting at the edge. Mark a line at this point and cut the rafter on the line.

2 HOLD THE RAFTER snug against the ridge board and mark the point where the rafter touches the top plate of the sidewall. Lay the framing square at this mark, as shown *above*, and outline the bird's mouth.

3 MARK A LINE parallel to the bird's mouth at a point 12 inches from the bottom of the bird's mouth. Cut the rafter on this line and cut out the bird's mouth. Test-fit the rafter, make any adjustments that are necessary, and use this rafter as a template to cut the remaining rafters.

4 CUT THE rake rafters in the same fashion, ¾ inch longer than the common rafters.

5 MEASURE FROM the intersection of the ridge and the header to the point where the sidewall meets the main roof rafters. Cut the valley rafters to length and miter the ends.

6 MEASURE SETS of jack rafters and miter-cut them to length.

7 TOENAIL ALL rafters into place with 10d nails. The rake rafters are face-nailed to the ridge and toenailed flush with the front of the top plates of the sidewalls.

8 SHEATH THE wall framing and the roof; then finish with roofing and siding, and install the window.

Building attic walls

Attic walls may be knee walls, straight partition walls, or sloped partition walls. Many projects include all three types. Build knee walls first, but before you start construction of any wall, strengthen the floor with additional joists, as necessary. Construction for each type of wall starts with determining where it will go.

Laying out a wall

Framing a partition wall is easiest if the wall location is directly under rafters or joists.

If the wall position doesn't fall right

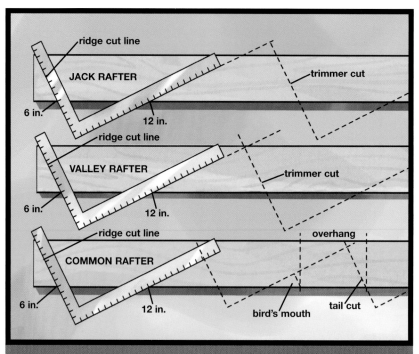

Marking and cutting rafters

Use a framing square and a tape measure to mark jack and valley rafters for cutting, as shown. Cut rake rafters 3/4 inch longer than common rafters.

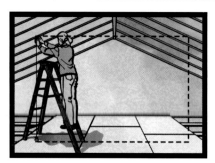

under rafters or joists, consider repositioning it; moving a few inches either way may not affect your plans. If the wall cannot be moved, install blocking by nailing lengths of 2×4 between the rafters or ceiling joists to provide something for you to nail the top plate to. Knee walls are built perpendicular to the rafters, so rafter location isn't an issue for them.

Use your attic floor plan to determine where the wall will go. Mark the location of the top plate on the joists or the blocking. Drop a plumb bob to the floor and mark both ends of the sill-plate position. Snap a chalk line between the marks and adjust the line to make sure the bottom plate lies square to the attic room.

Building knee walls

These short walls enclose the triangular area at the edge of the roof. Most building codes require knee walls to be of a specific minimum height; check codes before you build. You can build knee walls in place or preassemble them and set them into place (measure first, sagging rafters or other irregularities make the measurements inconsistent).

Lay out the wall location and then

measure the rafters-to-subfloor distance along the wall's length. If the measurements are consistent within ¼ inch, you can build an assembled wall (see page 122). The knee-wall top plate rests on studs cut to the angle of the roof. Scribe the angle on one stud, as shown, and use this stud as a template to mark the others. Assemble the wall on the attic floor, tilt it into place, and face-nail the studs to the sides of the rafters. Nail blocking between them.

If the rafter-to-floor distance varies by more than ¼ inch, you may be able to angle-cut the studs and force them into place under the rafters. Severe sagging may require new rafters or a remedy prescribed by an engineer.

Building a straight partition wall

The top plate of a straight partition wall runs flat from one side of the attic to the other. This wall can be erected only in an attic with enough clear space for the necessary 7-foot, 6-inch ceiling height. A straight wall is easier to build than one with a sloped ceiling. There is no variation in the height of the wall, so you can cut all the studs at once and to the same length.

After you have marked the location of the wall, use the methods shown on pages 122 and 124 to either build an assembled wall or build the wall in place.

If you build an assembled wall, you may be able to force its full length into place by pushing up the rafters. It's better to cut the studs ¼ inch shorter than the required length to allow the wall to clear the ceiling or joists and rafters. Shim the difference and nail through the ceiling to the joists.

Building a sloping partition wall

Most attic walls slope because few attics have sufficient height to allow for straight walls to the ceiling. Unlike straight walls, you must build sloped walls in place.

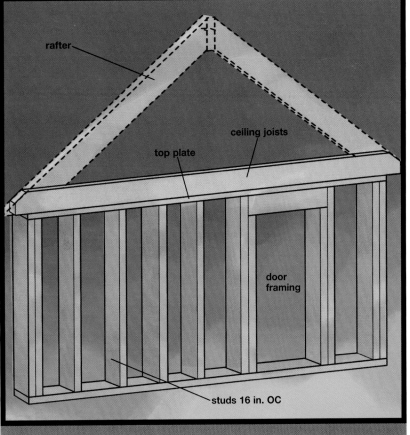

Building a straight partition wall

Straight partition walls are fairly easy to build: Mark the wall location on the floor and rafters, install the ceiling joists, and preassemble the wall or build it in place.

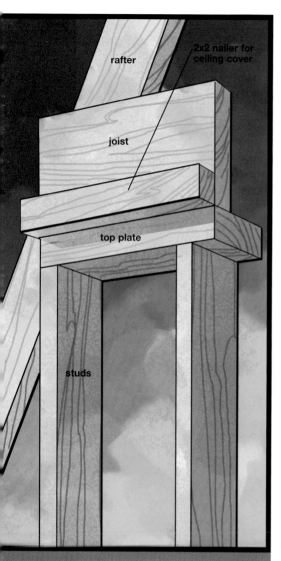

rafter

2x2 nailer for ceiling cover

joist

top plate

studs

Partition-wall support options

A partition wall is easier to frame if you locate it directly under rafters or ceiling joists *above*. Either build the wall in place or install a preassembled wall, fasten it to the joists, and add the nailer to support the ceiling material. Partition walls between rafters need blocking for support *right*. Install the joists first; then nail 2×4 blocking between them. Build the wall in place. Start with the 1×6 nailer for the ceiling; then install plates and studs.

Begin by marking the location of the wall's horizontal top plate and the wall's bottom plate. Mark the locations either on the rafters or on blocking installed between the rafters, if the location of the wall you're building requires them. Nail these plates in place. Then cut the sloping top plates to length and fasten them as well. Use a plumb bob to mark the top and bottom plates for 16-inch stud spacing and measure the length of each stud separately. Cut the studs at the angle of the roof and toenail them in place, checking them for plumb with a level as you go.

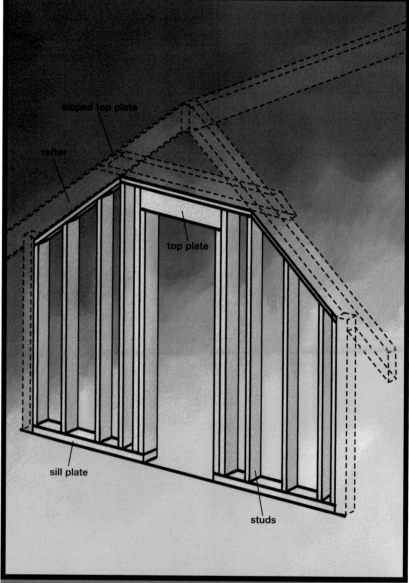

sloped top plate

rafter

top plate

sill plate

studs

Sloping partition walls

Sloping partition walls are more common and a bit more difficult to build, as you must build them in place and bevel the top of each rafter to fit the roof slope.

The task of installing windows and doorways in attics follows the same steps used in other areas in the house. Even though you have to work above ground on gable ends, attic installation is often easier.

Openings in partition walls

The installation of a window or door in an attic partition wall (or a doorway in a knee wall) is straightforward. Locate the wall opening, as dictated by your plan, and frame the opening for your window or door in the wall as you build it in place or preassemble it (see pages 121–124, and follow the instructions for attic wall construction on the previous pages). Then hang the door or window.

Openings in gable-end walls

Rafters and sidewalls support most of the weight of a roof, so gable-end walls are rarely load-bearing, which makes window and door installation easier. You don't have to build temporary support walls to cut new openings in non-load-bearing walls.

Attics often have a window in one or both end walls. Those windows usually provide decorative interest from the outside but little light or ventilation for the inside. On many older homes, most of these windows are old, single-paned, and poorly constructed. They're probably not right for your new room, but the framing for an old window opening may be suitable for installation of a new window.

If the framing is in good condition and the window is large enough and properly located for your plan, measure the rough opening and order an energy-efficient replacement unit (see page 166).

If the existing window is unsuitable, you can move or enlarge its opening. If no window exists, you can cut a new opening. You can use the same technique to install exterior attic doorways—to a second-story deck, for example. The only difference is that the opening is larger and the header construction is different. Follow the procedures outlined on page 166, altering them for doorways as appropriate.

replaced post with header and two posts

Be wary of ridge beams

Although gable-end walls are not usually load-bearing, there is one exception: a roof supported by a ridge beam. Ridge beams commonly support cathedral ceilings, transferring the weight normally borne by the sidewalls to the end walls of the structure. These beams are often made of heavy lumber, sometimes glued and laminated. If you have a cathedral ceiling or an unusually heavy central beam running the length of the house, inspect its construction carefully. It can be modified (as shown by the example *above*), but modifying it is expensive and requires professional advice. Consult with a structural engineer before going too far with your plans.

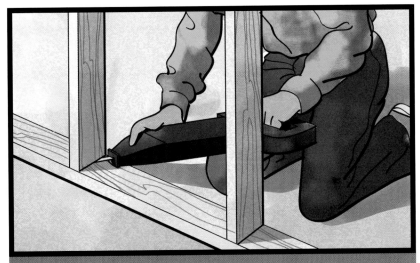

Removing gable-end studs

To remove studs in a gable-end wall, remove the top nails with a cat's paw, pry the studs loose from the siding with a flat bar, then cut the bottom nails, as shown.

If your attic remodeling involves adding or replacing windows, you'll be pleasantly surprised at the benefit-to-hassle ratio of installing them. They're not terribly difficult to put in, and big, bright windows in good working order are always a big plus.

1 TAKE OUT the interior wall surface (usually drywall or plaster) around the window opening; then test-fit the new window. Be sure to center it in the rough opening. Support the weight of the window with blocks and shims placed under the bottom jamb. Make sure the window is plumb and level, adjusting the shims, as necessary.

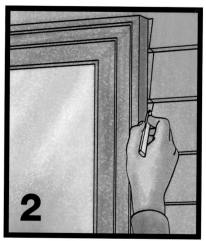

2 TRACE THE outline of the window molding on the exterior of the house. If you have vinyl or metal siding, enlarge the outline to accommodate the required extra J-channel moldings. Remove the window after you finish the outline.

3 CUT ALONG the outline with a reciprocating saw held at a shallow angle, or with a circular saw adjusted so the blade depth equals the thickness of the veneer or siding. Use a sharp chisel to complete the cuts at the corners.

4 CUT 8-inch-wide strips of building paper and slip them between

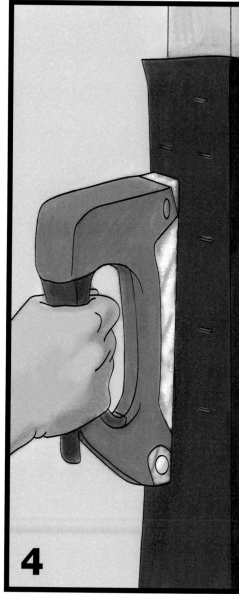

the siding and sheathing around the entire window opening. Wrap the paper around the framing members and staple it in place.

5 CUT A LENGTH of drip edge to fit over the top of the window, then slip it between the veneer or siding and building paper.

6 PLACE THE window into the opening, then push the molding firmly against the sheathing.

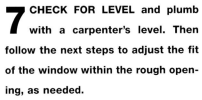

drip edge

5

7

8

7 CHECK FOR LEVEL and plumb with a carpenter's level. Then follow the next steps to adjust the fit of the window within the rough opening, as needed.

8 IF THE WINDOW is level, you're lucky. Simply pre-drill and nail both of the bottom corners of molding with 16d casing nails, then finish nailing the rest of the molding.

9

9 IF THE WINDOW is not level, which is more likely, especially in an older home, nail only the higher of the two bottom corners. Then have a helper adjust the shimming under the lower corner of the window from the inside of the house while you check for level on the outside. When the window is level, finish nailing.

Framing the opening
To frame a skylight opening, build a temporary support wall, then cut and frame the opening, doubling the support members on all sides.

Installing a curbed skylight

Build a square 2×4 curb, making it ⅜ inch smaller than the interior of the skylight, and toenail the curb to the roof. Flash the curb with step flashing on the sides and with collars on the top and bottom, working from bottom to top, so the pieces overlap to shed rain. Caulk the edge of the curb and set the skylight on it. Drive gasketed aluminum nails through holes in the flange and into the curb.

Most skylights are designed for do-it-yourself installation, but framing the opening requires some carpentry skills.

Laying out, framing, and cutting the opening

This part of skylight installation is similar to dormer preparation. Referring to the dormer instructions on pages 158–162, mark the opening, install support walls, and cut the rafters. Then frame in the opening, doubling the support members on all sides. Cut the opening and remove only enough shingles for the skylight to rest on the sheathing.

Installing a self-flashing skylight

Test-fit the skylight flange against the sheathing to make sure it lies flat around its entire surface. Coat the edges of the opening with roofing cement and lay the skylight in place with the bottom flange overlapping the shingles. Nail the top and side flanges with roofing nails at 6-inch intervals. Coat the flange entirely with roofing cement and replace the shingles from the bottom up.

Preventing leaks
Skylights call for careful installation to prevent possible leaks later. Follow installation instructions carefully and you'll be rewarded with a weathertight seal.

Installing insulation

Insulating your attic is one of the most cost-effective energy-saving moves you can make—doing so lowers the load on your heating and cooling system, and makes the space much more comfortable, summer and winter. Staple paper-faced batts to rafters as shown.

5 TUCK THE BATT or blanket into the rafter cavity, stapling batts every 6 inches. Hold blankets in place with chicken wire, wire netting, or tiger's teeth.

6 COVER THE ENTIRE SURFACE of unfaced insulation with a 6-mil polyethylene vapor barrier, stapling it to the rafters. Faced insulation forms its own vapor barrier.

Installing vents and insulation

Insulate the roof above your new attic room, not the floor below it. Also, if you don't use the space behind knee walls for storage, insulate the knee walls and any floor space behind them. If these areas will be used for storage, insulate only the roof above them.

Venting and insulation go together. Insulation loses its insulating ability when wet; venting lets moisture escape from insulation and helps keep the underside of the roof cooler.

Insulation baffles (sheets of corrugated hard plastic) are available in widths that fit 16- and 24-inch stud spacing. They allow free air passage between the insulation and the roof, and are used in conjunction with soffit and ridge vents.

Many older homes do not have rafters deep enough to accommodate the thickness of both insulation baffles and the batts or blankets. If your rafters are too narrow, add 2× furring to them before adding baffles and insulation.

1 TO INSULATE FLOORS under attic storage space, make baffles around recessed light fixtures and at the eaves directly above any vents. Toenail 1× baffles about 3 inches from each side of light fixtures to allow heat to escape. Nail baffles along top plates of sidewalls to keep batts from covering soffit vents and to allow air to travel upward along the underside of the sheathing.

2 START A ROLL of insulation at one edge at the eaves. Unroll it with the vapor-barrier side down, pushing it under any existing wiring and cutting it to fit around bridging. Insulate the eaves along one side of the attic; then do the other side. Then fill in the middle.

3 WHERE TWO ROLLS meet compress their ends slightly so they fit snugly against each other.

4 INSULATE THE ROOF NEXT. Place baffles between the rafters. Work from the bottom of the eaves to the roof peak.

Cutting fiberglass

Fiberglass batts or blankets are easy to cut. Use either of the following two methods:
• Lay a board along the cutting line and compress the insulation against a piece of plywood beneath. Cut the paper backing and fiberglass with a utility knife. (Use a sharp, new blade).
• Use an insulation knife. Actually just a utility knife fitted with a piece of curved plastic that looks like a hand guard, the knife works by compressing the insulation just before it reaches the blade. Insulation knives are faster and less cumbersome to use than the board method mentioned above.

Fiberglass safety

Fiberglass is made of thin glass fibers that release into the air when insulation is installed. The fibers can be extremely irritating to your lungs, eyes, and skin. Wear a respirator rated for fine dust, a long-sleeve shirt, long pants, gloves, safety goggles, and a hat when working with fiberglass. Or use a low-irritant fiberglass whose fiberglass batts are encapsulated in another material.

10

finishing touches

NOW THAT YOUR NEW SPACE IS BUILT, framed, plumbed, and wired, and all the doors and windows are framed in, it's time to finish the job. This is a particularly satisfying part of the process because the skeleton of space evolves into a fully formed finished room or suite of rooms. This chapter shows you how to estimate the amounts of materials you need—an essential skill. It also offers step-by-step instructions on how to install various flooring materials, including parquet or vinyl tile, laminate, sheet vinyl, and carpet. In addition, you'll discover the best methods for installing drywall and both sheet and board paneling, plus how to install a suspended ceiling. After all that, it's time for the finishing touches: the cabinetry, shelving, and trim that allow your project to function and look just as you envisioned.

OPPOSITE: At this point in the remodeling game, you can begin to reap the fruits of your labor. It's time to fill the barren shell of your new space with all the amenities that make it both functional and dream-worthy. Your choices of cabinetry, wallcovering, woodwork, floor covering, and a host of decorative items can make all the difference in transforming your space into something truly special.

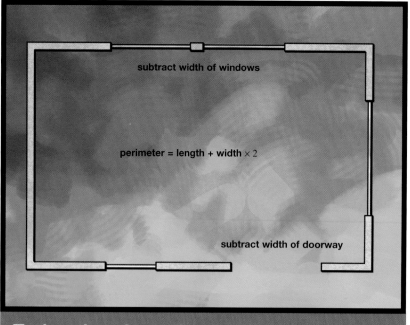

subtract width of windows

perimeter = length + width × 2

subtract width of doorway

Estimating drywall quantities

Measure the length and width of the room, disregarding any doors or other openings. Add the two measurements together, then multiply by two to determine the perimeter. Make deductions from your total, as shown here.

Estimating materials

FLOORING The first step in installing solid-wood flooring, carpeting, manufactured flooring, sheet flooring, or tile is to measure the floor and take your measurements to the flooring supplier, who then calculates the amounts of materials and supplies that you need.

DRYWALL To estimate the number of 4×8 drywall sheets you need, calculate the total length of the perimeter of the room, divide the result by four, and round up the answer to the nearest whole number. Deduct the sheet amounts shown in the illustration *above* for doors and windows, and round up the result to the nearest whole sheet. To estimate the number of sheets for a ceiling, divide the width of the room by 4 and the length by 8. Round up both numbers and multiply them together to get the number of sheets. Order a few extra sheets to allow for damage and cutting errors.

Installing parquet or vinyl tile

You'll need:

- Tape measure
- Chalk line
- Mastic trowel
- Marking pencil
- Hair dryer and utility knife (for resilient tile)
- Fine-toothed backsaw (for parquet tile)
- Knee pads
- Tiles
- Mastic
- Cork (for parquet tiles)
- 2x2 sheets of plywood (optional)

Most wood-parquet and resilient tile adheres to the floor with mastic, so installation methods are the same. The only differences are the types of mastic needed and the notch sizes of the trowels. Make sure the floor is properly prepared before you begin.

Tile layout

Although you can start your tile layout along any wall that is square to the room, laying out quadrants, as shown in the box *below*, allows you to center the design, leaving even spaces at the walls. For durability and appearance, arrange your layout so full tiles extend

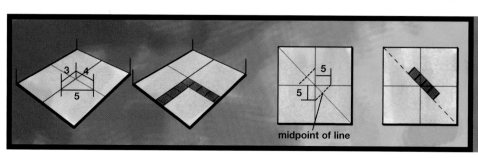

midpoint of line

Tile layout

Use chalk lines as shown to guide tile positioning. Then follow the step-by-step instructions *opposite* to tile the floor.

into doorways.

1 SNAP CHALK LINES at the midpoints of opposite walls. If the area is irregular, snap the chalk lines on the largest rectangular portion of the floor.

2 TEST FOR SQUARE. Make sure the intersection of the line makes a perfect right angle by using the 3-4-5 triangular method. Measure and mark a point 3 feet from the intersection on one axis and 4 feet from the intersection on the other axis. Now measure the distance between the two points. If it's exactly 5 feet, your lines are square. If the intersection is not square, adjust the lines until they meet at 90 degrees.

3 DRY-LAY THE TILES along the lines in both directions. Start with the line that runs to a doorway and slide the tile so you have a partial tile at the opening and equal spaces at least half a tile wide on opposite walls. Re-mark the final layout lines and test them again for square.

Setting the first quadrant

All adhesives have a specific open time—the amount of time that passes between spreading the adhesive until it starts to cure. Open time is marked on the packaging. Tiles don't adhere properly to adhesive after its open time has passed; apply only as much as you can cover in that time.

1 STARTING AT the intersection of your layout lines, put a small amount of adhesive on the floor. Then holding the trowel at a 30- to 45-

degree angle, spread the adhesive with the smooth edge of the trowel. Don't cover the layout lines. Strike a balance between spreading the adhesive too thick (which causes it to ooze out between the tiles) and spreading it too thin (which prevents a good bond). Then comb the adhesive into ridges with the notched side of the trowel.

2 SET THE FIRST TILE. Hold it by the edges and set a corner at the intersection of the layout lines. Lower the tile so it is in perfect alignment with the lines. Set the next few tiles along each axis in the same way, tilting the tongue of parquet tiles into the grooves as you set them into the adhesive. Then fill in the area between.

3 Set the tiles in place—don't slide them. Doing so gets mastic on their edges and faces. If you do get mastic on the surface of a set tile, wipe it immediately, but gently, with a rag dampened with the solvent specified by the manufacturer. Work carefully to keep each tile squarely aligned with the adjacent one. Minor errors grow into major ones as you lay subsequent tiles.

4 MARK AND CUT tiles when you reach walls or other obstructions as shown *above*. Cut parquet with a fine-toothed backsaw; warm resilient tiles with a hair dryer, then cut them with a utility knife.

Rolling the floor

When all the tiles have been set, finish the job by rolling the floor with a rented tile roller.

Self-stick tiles

If working with mastic sounds messy, smelly, and a bit intimidating, consider the alternative. Many manufacturers make resilient flooring in the form of self-stick tiles. Layout and installation are similar to the glue-down variety, except you don't have to trowel on adhesive, worry about open time, or work on one quadrant at a time because the adhesive sets immediately. You simply peel and stick them. The adhesives are durable; material quality can be as good as the glue-down variety. The only drawback is material cost. Self-stick tiles cost more than glue-down. If you're doing your first installation or, if you're looking for a fast, easy alternative to traditional tiling methods, the self-stick option is well worth considering.

Finishing the remaining quadrants

When the first quadrant is done, wait until the adhesive cures (see packaging for cure times) before laying the other quadrants. Or, if you don't want to wait, you can lay 2×2-foot pieces of plywood on the newly laid tiles and walk on them as you lay more tile. Start again in the center of the room and use the same installation methods for the remaining quadrants.

Don't walk directly on the tiles until the adhesive has cured. If you're laying parquet tiles, fill the gap at the walls with cork to keep them from shifting.

Floating a floor

You'll need:

- Tape measure
- Wax marking pencil
- Circular saw, radial arm saw, or table saw and power miter box
- Underlayment
- Flooring planks
- Installation kit (typically includes wall spacers, a pull bar, and a tapping block)

New manufactured or laminate flooring products don't have to be attached to the subfloor.

Laminate flooring materials consist of a tough synthetic layer bonded to medium-density fiberboard. The first generation of these materials was edge-glued together, a process that required careful attention to glue application, clamping, and prompt wiping up of extra glue that oozed out between planks. Too much glue resulted in a sticky line between planks; too little meant the planks absorbed water at the joints, swelled, and eventually crumbled and deteriorated.

A second generation of the same product allows for glueless installation. Planks simply snap together, cutting installation time roughly in half. Special tongue-and-groove designs, some coated with a sealant to improve water-resistance, make for tight, even joints. Although initially designed for do-it-yourselfers, many professional installers prefer these products as well, citing speedy installation, fewer callbacks for failed joints, and the fact that customers can use their floor the same day it is installed, rather than waiting for glue to dry. An additional benefit: Most glueless floors can be disassembled and reassembled up to three times (consult individual manufacturer's product literature), which means you literally can take it with you if you move. For most laminate floor applications, glueless flooring is a natural

Installing a floating floor

Roll out the underlayment and lay the first course against half inch spacers placed around the perimeter of the room. The spacers ensure that the floor has room to expand and contract with changes in temperature and humidity.

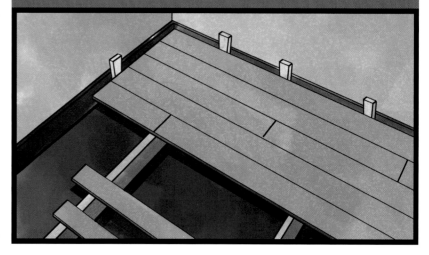

choice. If the pattern, brand, dimension, or material you want is only available in materials that require gluing, follow the package instructions carefully, and use the manufacturer's glue.

Installing the underlayment

Start in a corner and butt the end of the underlayment—often a roll of sheet foam—against one wall. Unroll it to the opposite wall and cut the end to fit. Some manufacturers recommend installing a section of flooring after laying the first course of underlayment. If that's what your directions recommend, alternately lay underlayment and flooring.

Otherwise continue unrolling the underlayment until you cover the entire floor surface. Butt the pieces together; don't overlap them. Tape the seams together unless the manufacturer says otherwise. For solid-panel underlayment, follow the manufacturer's instructions. Solid panels usually require a ¼-inch gap for expansion.

Laying the planks

1 SET THE FIRST COURSE against spacers (provided in the product's installation kit) along the wall.

2 SNAP OR TAP the planks together using the technique specified in the package directions and the tapping block and pull bar provided in the installation kit.

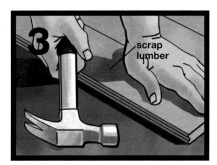

3 LAY THE PLANKS from one side-wall to the other, marking the last plank so you can cut it to fit. Transfer the mark to the back of the plank and cut the plank using a circular saw, table saw, or radial arm saw with a fine-tooth, carbide-tipped blade. Turn the plank facedown when using a circular saw or radial arm saw, faceup when using a table saw. Snap this plank in place and use the pull bar to snug the boards.

4 MEASURE FROM the opposite wall to both ends of the first course and to the middle. Divide all three measurements by the width of a plank; if you have a remainder of more than 2 inches, lay two more rows, following the manufacturer's instructions for staggering the end joints.

5 IF THE RESULT of the division doesn't leave at least a 2-inch plank on the opposite wall, split the difference, disassemble the first course, and trim the planks narrower, so you have at least 2 inches of material along the starting and ending walls. Continue laying courses, starting each row with the piece left over from the previous course (if it is more than 1 foot long.

Lay the last course

Set the first plank of the last course along the edge of the wall and mark its width. Transfer the mark to the back of the plank and rip it with a circular saw. Mark and cut each succeeding plank the same way. Don't cut planks all the same width unless you know the wall is square to the floor. Snap or tap the planks in place.

Installing sheet vinyl

You'll need:

- Scissors
- Kraft, butcher, or felt paper
- Duct tape
- Steel straightedge
- Water-soluble marker
- Grease pencil (for installing glossy flooring)
- Utility knife
- ¼-inch notched trowel
- Floor roller
- Staple gun and staples
- Flooring material
- Adhesive
- Seaming solvent

Sheet-vinyl flooring comes in two types: One is installed with adhesive spread on the entire floor, the other with adhesive at the edges only.

Unroll the sheet in a different room so it relaxes at room temperature for several hours before you cut it. While it adjusts to the environment of your home, cut a paper template that you'll use to cut the flooring.

Cutting a template

A paper template is a full-sized pattern that you use to cut the sheet flooring to fit the room.

1 COVER THE PERIMETER of the room to within ¼ inch of walls and obstacles with pieces of kraft paper, heavy butcher paper, or 15-pound felt paper. The heavier the paper, the less it moves around as you work. The template doesn't have to fit the room precisely because baseboards and shoe moldings will cover the edges.

2 OVERLAP THE EDGES of the paper by 2 inches and tape them with duct tape. Then cut out small triangles through the paper every 2 feet

or so. Put tape over the triangles to hold the template to the subfloor below.

3 HOLD A long straightedge on the edge of the paper and mark its perimeter on the subfloor with a water-soluble marker. This line shows you where to set the sheet vinyl when you bring it into the room.

4 ROLL UP the template carefully and move it into the room where you left the sheet.

Trimming a vinyl sheet

1 ADJUST ANY PIECES that will be seamed so the pattern lines match before laying the template on the vinyl. Overlap the edges by 3 inches at the seams. Tape the edges of the seam together so they won't move. Then lay out the template on the flooring, making sure the template lies on the sheet in the way the sheet will be installed in the room.

2 LINE UP the edges of the template with the pattern lines, if possible. That way, the lines don't look awkward in doorways or along prominent walls. Shift the template on the sheet until it's square to the pattern.

3 TAPE THE TEMPLATE to the sheet vinyl through the triangular holes and mark its edge on the vinyl with a water-soluble marker (use a grease pencil if the surface is glossy).

4 ROLL UP the template and dispose of it.

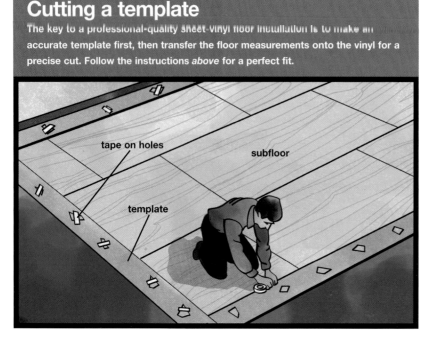

Cutting a template

The key to a professional-quality sheet-vinyl floor installation is to make an accurate template first, then transfer the floor measurements onto the vinyl for a precise cut. Follow the instructions *above* for a perfect fit.

tape on holes

subfloor

template

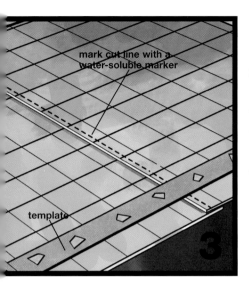

mark cut line with a water-soluble marker

template

3

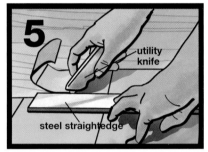

utility knife

steel straightedge

5 CUT THE EDGES of the sheet vinyl with a utility knife and a steel straightedge pressed against the material. When you're done, roll up the vinyl (don't fold it) with the pattern side in and take it to the room where you will install it.

6 STARTING ALONG the wall with the fewest obstacles, unroll the sheet and slide it under door casings. Tug and shift it into place.

Gluing the sheet

Gluing techniques vary with the type of material you install. Perimeter-bond sheet vinyl is glued around the edges of the sheet only. Full-spread materials are glued to the entire floor surface. Follow the directions that correspond to the material you have.

Perimeter-bond gluing

1 START AT A CORNER. Pull back on an edge along a wall, exposing about 8 inches of subfloor, or as much as the manufacturer recommends.

2 SPREAD A BAND of adhesive on the exposed subfloor using a ¼-inch notched trowel. If you cross a seam, stop spreading the adhesive about 18 inches from the seam line.

3 EASE THE EDGE of the sheet onto the adhesive and roll it with a floor roller. Then pull back the other edges of the sheet and repeat the procedures along each wall.

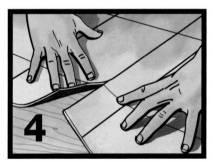

4

4 SEAM THE SHEET, as shown above.

5 STAPLE THE EDGES to the subfloor, if required, keeping the staples close to the wall so the base trim will hide them.

Full-spread vinyl

1 CAREFULLY FOLD half the sheet back without creasing it.

2 SPREAD ADHESIVE with a ¼-inch notched trowel, working from the corner to the center until you cover the exposed subfloor. Stop applying adhesive about 18 inches from any seam lines.

3 FOLD BACK THE SHEET onto the adhesive and roll it from the center to the edges. Then adhere the other half of the floor following the same procedures.

Seaming sheet vinyl

Follow these steps to seam a sheet.

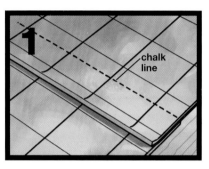

1

chalk line

1 SNAP A CHALK LINE down the center of the seam overlap.

utility knife

2

2 CUT BOTH LAYERS of vinyl along the seam line. Don't cut one layer at a time—you'll leave gaps.

3 PULL BACK both edges of the sheet vinyl and apply adhesive to the floor. Then press both sides of the seam into the adhesive. Clean any adhesive residue off the seam.

4 WHEN THE SEAM has set, seal it with seaming solvent, which fuses the edges together.

installing carpet

Installing conventional carpet

You'll need:

TOOLS

- Hammer
- Tape measure
- Tin snips
- Utility knife
- Straightedge
- Screwdriver
- Stapler and staples (for installation on wood subfloor)
- Marking pencil or marker
- Chalk line
- Scissors
- Duct tape
- Double-sided carpet tape (for installation on concrete)
- Hotmelt seaming tape

RENTED TOOLS

- Row cutter
- Seaming iron
- Knee kicker
- Power stretcher
- Carpet trimmer
- Stair tool

Conventional carpet has a fiber backing and requires you to install a pad under it. The carpet is stretched during installation, then held in place by tackless strips nailed along the edge of the floor. Homeowners often hire professional installers to lay carpet, but you can do it yourself. A few things you need to consider before taking on the job: Large pieces of carpet are heavy and awkward, stretching carpet requires adequate muscle, making an error in measuring or cutting can be costly; and failing to stretch carpet tightly results in a sloppy-looking job.

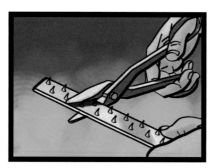

TACKLESS STRIP is a thin strip of plywood with very sharp, pointed teeth embedded in it. The teeth, which protrude from the top of the tackless strip and point toward the wall, hold the carpet in place. Installing it is the first step in laying carpet. Start in a corner and nail the strip all around the edges of the room, leaving a gap at the wall equal to two-thirds of the carpet thickness. Cut the strips with tin snips and fasten them to the subfloor with at least two nails per section of strip.

Padding a floor

1 UNROLL A STRIP of pad and cut it with a utility knife.

2 STAPLE THE PAD every 6–12 inches on a wood subfloor. For concrete surfaces, tape the carpet with double-faced carpet tape along

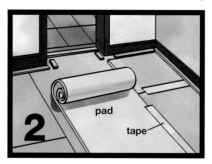

pad

tape

its edges.

3 BUTT SUCCEEDING STRIPS and tape the joints with duct tape.

4 TRIM THE PAD ¼ inch back from the tackless strip to keep it from riding over the strip when the carpet is stretched.

Cutting the carpet

1 FOR LOOP-PILE CARPET, use a screwdriver to mark a cutting path and cut from the face side with a utility knife. Cut all other types of carpet from the back.

2 MEASURE THE PIECE you are planning to lay first and mark each cut on the face of the carpet.

3 ROLL BACK THE CARPET and snap a chalk line.

4 CUT THE CARPET with a utility knife held firmly against a steel straightedge. Cut just deep enough into the carpet to sever the backing. Pull the two pieces of carpet apart carefully, so as not to pull carpet fibers out of the backing. Snip unseparated carpet fibers with scissors.

The rough fit

1 MEASURE AND CUT carpet sections, leaving a 4- to 6-inch surplus along each wall and a 3-inch

leave 3-inch overlap at seam

overlap at seams.

2 SQUARE THE SECTIONS to the room and slit the corners so they lie flat. Now you're ready to seam the carpet and stretch it.

Seaming carpet

1 FOR LOOP-PILE CARPET, first align the seam edges parallel to each other. Place a straightedge on the edge of the top section and cut the bottom piece with a row cutter. Cut the surplus at the wall with a utility knife.

2 FOR OTHER CARPET STYLES, fold back the overlap and snap a chalk line on the back of the carpet at the seam edges. Cut along the chalk line with a utility knife and straightedge.

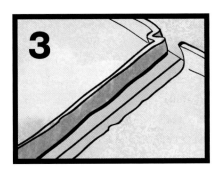

3 CUT HOTMELT seaming tape to the exact length of the seam and center the tape under the seam, adhesive side up.

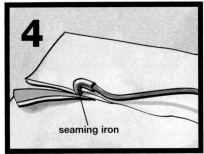

seaming iron

4 SLIP THE SEAMING IRON onto the tape at one end of the carpet and let both sides flop onto the iron. Glide the iron slowly along the tape, pressing the seam edges together behind it as you go.

5 WHEN YOU REACH the wall, stop and let everything cool for 10 minutes. Then roll back the surplus carpet to expose the unheated tape. Heat the tape and finish the seam by cutting off stray backing or loose pile ends with scissors.

Stretching carpet

1 CARPET STRETCHERS must be adjusted before you use them. Adjust the bite of both the knee kicker and the power stretcher until the teeth just grab the backing without poking through it.

2 TO USE THE KNEE KICKER, bite its head into the carpet about 1 inch from the wall. Push down on the handle and give the cushion a swift kick with your knee. Push down the surplus carpet at the wall with a hammer and a stair tool.

3 TO USE THE POWER STRETCHER, set the head about 6 inches away from the wall and adjust the extension tubes so the foot pushes against a piece of 2x4 (long enough to

span three studs) at the other wall. Press the lever until the lever locks.

4 BEGIN STRETCHING in a corner by an entrance and proceed along both sides of the opening for about 3 feet.

5 POWER-STRETCH one corner at a time, knee-kicking along each length in turn. Follow the manufacturer's directions for the type of equipment you rent.

Self-stick carpet squares

If you want to install carpet yourself but don't want the strain, hassle, and risk of stretching conventional carpet, self-stick carpet squares may be the ticket. They are self-backing, so you don't need a pad, and installation is similar to self-stick resilient tile (see page 174). In addition, carpet squares are generally comfortable, durable, and neat-looking.

Because the product is primarily sold for commercial use, you may have to inquire at carpet specialty shops and wholesalers to locate the product. Be forewarned—you won't find luxurious, deep-pile varieties or a broad selection of colors. For that reason, self-stick carpet is best for informal spaces, such as family rooms, where a firm, low-nap surface is best.

If you're looking for a long-wearing surface that's quiet, easy-to-clean, and hides minor surface imperfections, it's well worth considering.

One other advantage worth mentioning: Unlike regular carpet, self-stick carpet is easily repaired. Just peel up the damaged tile according to the manufacturer's instructions and replace it with a new tile. Order a few extra tiles just incase.

installing drywall

Trimming

1 TRIM CARPET edges with a wall trimmer rather than a utility knife. Adjust the trimmer according to carpet thickness.

2 START AT the lapped end of the material and slice downward at an angle until the trimmer is flat against the floor.

3 HOLD THE TRIMMER against both the wall and the floor and plow along the edge of the wall.

4 TRIM THE last few inches with a utility knife and tuck the trimmed edge into the gap with a hammer and a stair tool.

Installing drywall

You'll need:

- Drywall tools (see page 103)
- Hammer or drill-driver
- Drywall sheets and tape

trap square with foot

cut backing after breaking

- Metal corner bead
- Drywall mud
- 1¼-inch drywall nails or screws
- Construction adhesive and caulking

Drywall installation is not technically complex, but you will be able to do a better job if you learn some basic techniques. The most difficult thing about working with drywall is that it is heavy and unwieldy. Many older homes are out of square, so cutting and fitting drywall can be a challenge. Professionals achieve a smooth surface after three compound applications and sandings, so you may want to count on four or five.

Before you begin, study the framing to be sure you can attach the drywall at all points. If you don't use adhesive, install two nails into the wall studs at 16-inch intervals and a single nail every 7 inches along edges. When using adhesive, apply a bead of drywall mastic to each stud. Drive nails or screws into the sheet at 18- to 24-inch intervals to hold the sheet in place while the

adhesive sets up. Keep adhesive 6 inches away from the tops and bottoms of the drywall sheets. When using screws, use a screw gun with an adjustable clutch or a variable-speed drill with a dimpler attachment. Both the clutch and the dimpler are designed to drive screws just below the surface without breaking the paper. Space screws 12 inches apart.

1 CUT ACROSS a sheet of drywall by first laying the sheet on scrap lumber to keep it off the floor, finished side facing up. Mark the sheet ¼ inch shorter than the measured length. Stand the drywall on edge and set your drywall square in place. Clasp the square firmly on top and press your toe against the bottom of the blade of the square to be sure it doesn't move. With the blade against the square, make a ⅛-inch-deep cut downward, and then finish by cutting up from the bottom. Snap back the cut segment away from the cut and then slice through the backing paper.

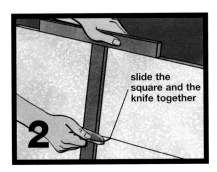

slide the square and the knife together

2 CUT ALONG the length of a sheet of drywall by setting the drywall square on the edge of a sheet and holding the knife against it at the correct spot. Slide the square along as you keep the knife in position. If the rip cut must be wider at one end, chalk a line and cut it freehand.

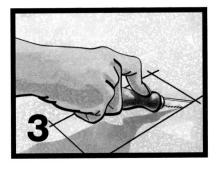

3 MAKE A HOLE for an electrical receptacle box by measuring from the box's edges to the edges of the adjacent sheets of existing drywall. Transfer measurements to the new sheet and draw a rectangle. Score the outline with a utility knife and cut the hole with a drywall saw. Or, for faster cuts, use a spiral saw.

4 CUT A HOLE for a pipe by measuring and marking the sheet for the center of the pipe. Draw a circle and cut it out with a drywall saw, hole saw, or spiral saw. Some spiral saws have hole-cutting jigs that work like a compass; in that case all you have to

do is mark the center of the pipe and set the jig to cut a hole of the proper diameter. Bore small holes with a power drill.

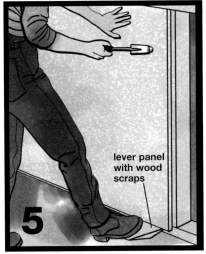

lever panel with wood scraps

5 INSTALL SHEETS horizontally by butting the upper sheets firmly against the ceiling. Cut sheets to lengths that fall midway across a stud. Snap a chalk line at stud locations along each sheet to show where to install the fasteners. Butt the lower panels firmly against the upper panels, tapered edge to tapered edge.

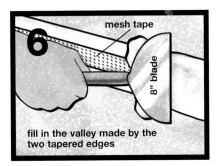

mesh tape

8" blade

fill in the valley made by the two tapered edges

6 FINISH THE DRYWALL by taping and mudding the joints. Press the mesh tape in place. Load an 8- or 10-inch taping knife with joint compound. Make sure the knife blade

more than spans the valley created by the tapered edges of the drywall. Fill in the taper only so you create a flat wall surface. For butt joints feather out the compound 8 to 10 inches on each side. If you end up with a small ridge in the middle of the joint, sand it off after the compound dries.

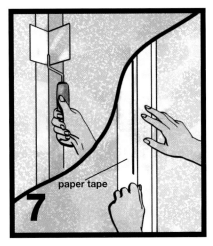

paper tape

7 FINISH INSIDE CORNERS by applying compound to both sides of the corner with a 6-inch blade. Cut a piece of paper tape, fold along its crease, and pat it into the corner. Run a corner blade down its length to embed the tape. In spots where it doesn't adhere, lift the tape, add compound, and embed. Feather later coats with a 10-inch taping knife.

Drywall nailing 101

Driving nails through drywall into the studs is harder than you might think. If you simply drive in a nail flush, you won't be able to cover it with joint compound. If you drive it too deeply, you'll break the drywall paper. If the paper is broken, the nail won't hold; it tears right through the inner core of gypsum.

installing
wall paneling

Installing paneling

You'll need:

- Tape measure
- Marking pencil
- Circular saw with plywood blade or fine-toothed handsaw
- Hammer
- Nail set
- 48-inch level
- Plumb bob
- Compass or scribing tool
- Caulking gun (if using construction adhesive)
- Sheet or board paneling
- Concrete sealer, 6-mil polyethylene (for installation over concrete walls)
- Construction adhesive (optional)
- 1×3 furring strips
- Finishing nails
- 8d nails

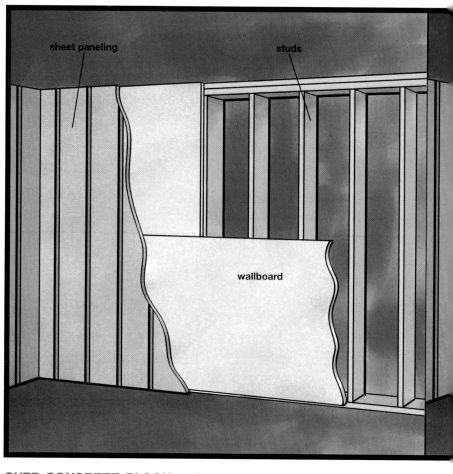

sheet paneling · studs

wallboard

Wood and hardboard paneling offers more design choices than many other wall finishings and is easy to install. Here's how:

Preparing for sheet paneling

CHECK THE WALL for level with a 4-foot level. If all areas are within ¼ inch of the same plane, you can proceed. If not, nail 1×2s every 24 inches at points where the panels will join.

EXPOSED STUDS must be covered before you can hang thin paneling. Hang ½-inch drywall to provide a solid surface. Or if local codes allow, use a thicker kind of paneling that's designed to be nailed directly to studs.

OVER CONCRETE BLOCK, seal the surface with a concrete sealer, cover the block with 6-mil polyethylene sheets, and attach 1×3 furring strips, as shown *above right*, shimming them to keep the surface level.

Installing sheet paneling

1 **ACCLIMATE THE PANELS to** your home by bringing them inside and storing them flat on the floor for several days before hanging. Failing to do so results in buckling or bowing.

2 **INSTALL THE FIRST PANEL** in an unobstructed corner, plumbing it with a 4-foot level and centering it on

a stud or furring strip. Fasten the panel every 8 inches with finishing nails that penetrate the studs or furring strips by at least ¾ inch. If you're using panel adhesive, run a bead on every nailing surface. Following the manufacturer's instructions, hang the panel, nailing at top and bottom.

3 **WHEN YOU MEET** an obstruction, such as a window, door, or corner of the room that is not plumb, butt the panel against the obstruction, overlapping another panel already in place. Use a compass or scribing tool to mark the outline of the obstruction; plan the width of the cut so the edge of the panel butts up against the adjacent panel.

board paneling

batten

wallboard

sealer

concrete block wall

vapor barrier

4 CUT THE PANEL using a fine-tooth blade (12 teeth to the inch for a handsaw; a plywood blade for a power saw) to avoid tearing up the edges. Cut paneling faceup with a handsaw or table saw, facedown with a radial arm or circular saw.

Installing tongue-and-groove paneling

1 ON A FINISHED WALL, nail 1×3 battens at the top and bottom of the wall and at 32 and 64 inches from the floor.

2 ON AN EXPOSED STUD WALL, snap chalk lines across the studs at the batten locations. With a circular saw set to 1½ inches and a chisel, form recesses in the studs for 1×3 battens. Nail the battens with 8d nails flush with the surface of the studs. Then mark the locations of battens on adjacent walls and cover them with ½-inch drywall.

3 ACCLIMATE THE BOARDS by bringing them into the room and laying them out for three days to a week. Failing to do so could result in warped or buckled paneling.

4 HANG THE FIRST BOARD plumb, scribing it, if necessary. Nail through the face of the board and into the battens with the tongue out. Then nail through the tongue at a 45-degree angle. Fit the groove of the next board into the tongue and tap it snug with a piece of panel scrap. Then nail the tongue. Check for plumb at every third board until you reach the opposite wall.

5 INSTALL THE LAST BOARD by measuring from the inside wall to the inside of the tongue of the next-to-last board. Now hold the last board to the wall, keeping it plumb, and set your compass to the distance between the mark and the wall. Scribe along the entire length of the board; cut along that line. Test-fit the board and cut the rear edge of the groove, if necessary, so the board falls in place. Nail through the face of the last board to the battens.

installing a dropped ceiling

Installing a dropped ceiling

You'll need:

- Tape measure
- Chalk line
- Line level, water level, and 4-foot level or laser level
- Drill-driver
- Tin snips
- Utility knife
- Wall molding
- Main runners
- Cross tees
- Edge runner
- Hanging wire
- Screws
- Screw eyes
- Acoustical tiles

A dropped ceiling (also called a suspended ceiling) consists of a metal grid and the acoustic tiles it supports. The grid hangs from the overhead framing. It consists of an edge runner, which is installed around the perimeter of the space; main runners, which run across the space; and cross tees, which go between the main runners. Depending on the tiles you choose, the main runners are spaced 24 or 48 inches on center. The cross tees are also placed to fit the tiles.

Dropped ceilings have several advantages. First they require no taping or mudding (so installing one generates no dust). Second they allow access to the space above, which works well in a basement where plumbing valves or electrical junction boxes are located. Third the space above them makes a

handy wiring chase for running wires with a minimum of fuss. Some newer tile designs imitate painted wood, plaster relief, and tin. Some are paintable. Before you start, insulate cold water pipes to prevent drips from condensation, which discolors the tiles.

1 DRAW A FLOOR PLAN, then measure the ceiling height. Most grid systems require at least 3 inches above to get the panels into place. Make sure the grid is low enough to clear things hanging from the joists, such as pipes, but high enough to clear the tops of windows and doorways (at least 7½ feet above the finished floor).

2 SLIP A LINE LEVEL onto your chalk line and adjust the line. Snap a level line around the perimeter of the room to indicate the top of the wall molding. Double-check your line for level with a 4-foot level. Or use a water level. If you have a large

room, you might want to rent a rotary laser level to establish a level line around the perimeter of the room. Do not look into the laser. To make sure you don't, snap chalk lines along the laser's path instead of leaving it running while you install the wall molding.

3 INSTALL THE EDGE support to the studs with its top edge even with the snapped lines. Butt the pieces together to make longer runs.

4 MARK THE EDGE support at the dimensions of the tile inserts (usually 2×2 or 2×4) and run a level string from one wall to the other at the bottom of the edge supports.

5 MEASURE THE LENGTH for the main supports at each mark (they may be different lengths at different locations) and cut them with snips. As you cut the main supports, make sure the slots for the cross members line up with the dimensions

of your inserts.

6 SUSPEND THE MAIN runners from screw eyes and wires (or whatever hardware is supplied with the materials) looped through holes in the runner flange. Tighten the wire so the runner is level with the string along its entire length.

7 INSTALL THE CROSS runners and measure the diagonals of each section to make sure they are square. If any section is out of square, snip off a section of the cross runner and bring it into alignment.

8 TILT THE TILE inserts into the opening of the grid, set one edge on a runner, and let the insert fall into place. Push the perimeter pieces snug against the tile.

Installing wall cabinets

You'll need:

- Tape measure
- Marking pencil
- Carpenter's level
- Drill-driver and 3-inch screws
- C-clamps
- Circular saw
- Hammer
- Chisel
- Toe-kick
- Cabinets
- Long, straight 2×4
- Stepladder

Successful wall-cabinet installation depends on good preparation. Smooth and prime all wall and ceiling surfaces, and install flooring. Draw lines to show the location of each stud. Carefully mark the location of each cabinet on the walls. Allow for small spacers at the corners so you don't have to cram the cabinets in too tightly.

If you purchased your cabinets ready-made, inspect them carefully. It's not unusual to find imperfections, and you won't be able to return them after you drive screws into them.

You also need to take a good look at your walls and floor. If your walls are not plumb or square and your floor is not level, you may end up with cabinets that don't fit. Check in advance and, if necessary, reposition your layout carefully and accordingly.

When you actually start the installation, you'll need a helper and a stable stepladder on hand. One person can hold a cabinet in perfect alignment, and the other can drive the screws. If the cabinets are very heavy, remove the doors and shelves to lighten the weight and reduce the chances of damaging the cabinets or injuring yourself.

stud locations

1 MARK THE WALL to show where each cabinet will go. Draw lines with a pencil to show the stud locations. (Draw lines lightly wherever your marks will not be covered by a cabinet.)

2 SECURE A STRAIGHT 2×4 with its top edge at the point where you want the bottom of your cabinets to be. Level the 2×4 and attach it with just a few screws or nails so you don't create a big wall-patching job when you remove it. Or use a T-brace, as shown *above right.*

3 BEGIN ATTACHING CABINETS in a corner. While a helper holds the cabinet, check for plumb in both directions. Use shims, as necessary. Once the cabinet is positioned, drive 2½- to 3-inch screws through the top and bottom framing pieces and into

T-brace

the wall studs. If your cabinet has a lip on top, drive the screws into it so the screws don't show. If you like, use trim or finish washers for a more finished look on the inside of the cabinet. Some manufacturers supply plastic screw-head covers.

4 INSTALL EACH CABINET flush with the next one, not only along its face but also at the top. Clamp them in place before fastening. Drill pilot holes and countersink them; then drive screws to hold the units together firmly.

5 INSTALL A SPACER where the last cabinet meets a sidewall. Hold the cabinet in place and measure for a spacer. Cut the spacer and attach it, using clamps to hold it firmly while you drill pilot holes and drive screws from the cabinet into the spacer. Then remove the clamps and attach the cabinet to the wall.

6 IN AN INSIDE CORNER attach a spacer to one of the cabinets to provide room for each cabinet door to open fully; then attach the other cabinet to the spacer. Drill pilot holes in the spacer and the adjacent cabinet frame. Then drive screws through the spacer and into the frame. Tighten the screws until the pieces fit together snugly, showing no gaps.

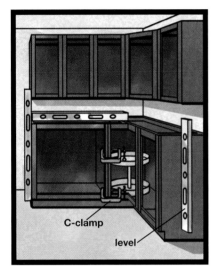

C-clamp

level

Base cabinets

Find the highest point of your floor using a level and a long 2×4. (Sight down its length to make sure that it's not bowed.) Set the board upright on the narrow side of its length. Place a carpenter's level in the center on top of the board. Raise one end or the other until the bubble is centered between the two lines.

Slide the board around the floor until you are sure you have found the high point. Level the board from this high point and measure the distance from the floor to the bottom of the raised end of the board to see how far out of level the floor is. Start installation at the highest point; you can shim the cabinets up but not down.

1 FIND THE HIGHEST POINT on your floor (method described

above). Set the first cabinet in place and check it for level in both directions. Make sure the stiles, or door faces, are plumb. Use shims at the floor to level and solidly support the cabinets. If your wall is out of plumb or wavy, you may need to shim the back of the cabinet as well.

2 DRIVE SCREWS through the back of the first cabinet frame into the wall studs. When possible screw through solid framing pieces. After driving the screws check to see whether the cabinet is still sitting flat on the floor. If not, back out the screws and adjust the shims before driving the screws back in. Check for level and plumb again.

3 USE CLAMPS, as shown *left,* to hold the next cabinet firmly in alignment. While you join the cabinets together, face frames and top edges flush. Use screws of a length that hold the cabinets firmly together but aren't so long they poke through the stiles. To keep the surface of the stiles smooth, drill pilot and countersink holes; then drive the screws. Most of the time you can use a hammer and chisel to nip off protruding shims. If you layer shims, cut them with a handsaw.

4 AT THE INSIDE CORNERS make a filler piece to fit snugly between the cabinet and the wall at both the top and the bottom and position it flush with the cabinet face. Drill pilot and countersink holes and drive in screws. If the filler piece is more than 4 inches wide, it must be attached to the wall.

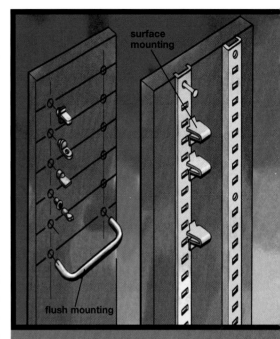

surface mounting

flush mounting

Shelving options

When installing shelves in an open or framed bookcase or hanging them as built-in units, you have a number of choices on how to support them. For fixed-height permanent shelving, you can cut dadoes in the sides and back of the unit. For movable shelves install surface or flush-mounted brackets, rear-mounted standards, or drill evenly spaced holes for removable clips or dowels. If you drill support holes, use this trick to ensure accurate alignment: Clamp a piece of pegboard over the piece to be drilled, and drill through the pegboard holes into the material to ensure uniform placement. Use a drill press or hand drill with a drill guide to ensure the holes are straight and of the correct depth.

5 IF YOUR FLOOR is out of level, gently pry off a preinstalled toe-kick and reinstall it flush to the floor. If the toe-kick was not preinstalled, simply nail it back on the cabinet with its lower edge flush to the floor. Or install a vinyl cove base.

Case molding

You'll need:

- ■ Tape measure
- ■ Marking pencil
- ■ Hammer and finish or casing nails
- ■ Utility knife
- ■ Clamps
- ■ Miter box and back saw
- ■ Plank and sawhorses or articulated ladder

Case molding—the trim that goes around doors and windows—gives a room a finished look.

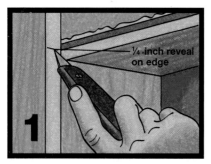

1 WORK CLOCKWISE when installing molding around a door or
window. Make a straight cut off the
bottom of the first vertical piece
straight, set the piece in place, and
mark the top for a miter cut. Hold the
piece in place and mark it with a
knife. For window and door casings,
take into account the ¼-inch reveal
on the edge of the jamb. As a guide
use a compass set to ¼ inch to mark
the reveal on the jamb.

2 CUT THE MITER by holding the
molding tightly against the back
of the miter box. Or use a power miter
saw or radial arm saw.

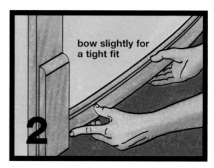

3 DRILL PILOT HOLES and tack
the first piece in place. Then
work on the top piece: Cut a piece of
trim with a miter at one end to fit
against the vertical piece you just
installed. Fit the miters together,
mark and miter the other end, and
tack the top molding in place.
Measure and miter the second vertical piece of trim and fit it to the top
piece. Doors are finished at this
point; around a window, you still need
to measure and miter the bottom
piece, and tack it into place.

4 FACE-NAIL THE LAST PIECE.
Drill pilot holes through the top
edge of each corner into the ends of
the verticals. Nail the joints, countersink the nails, and fill the nail holes.

Base molding

Install all door and window casings
before you begin installing the base
molding, which covers the bottom
perimeter of walls. After the base
molding is in, install quarter round, or
base shoe. Cut the first piece to length
with a regular 90-degree cut so it butts
against the adjacent wall. To cope the
overlapping piece, make an inside 45-
degree miter cut. Use a coping saw to
cut away the excess wood along the
molding profile.

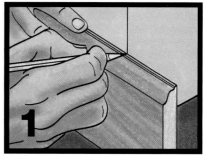

1 HOLD AND MARK the pieces in
place. For an outside corner, butt
one end of the molding in place, letting the other end extend past the
corner of the wall. Make the mark
exactly even with the corner.

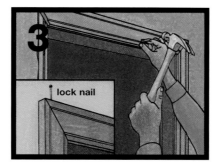

2 CUT THE PIECE about ¹⁄₁₆ inch
longer than the space. Make
sure any casing is well secured so it
doesn't move when you press against
it. Push the baseboard in place by
bending it into position to create a
tight fit on both sides. Nail molding
into place and fill the holes.

Crown molding

Use a plank and two sturdy sawhorses
to make a platform to stand on while
installing the molding, or use an articulated ladder (see pages 110–113).
Have a helper hold the molding while
you measure, position, and fasten it.

Before you begin this challenging
project, review the following:

1 USE A STEEL measuring tape (rather than cloth or wood) to get the most accurate measurements. Use a V, not a line, and use an extra-sharp pencil to make all markings. When measuring, allow for the opening left in the blade's wake, called the kerf, usually about ⅛ inch wide. If you're making just one cut, account for the kerf by marking the waste side of the cutoff line with an X to avoid confusion.

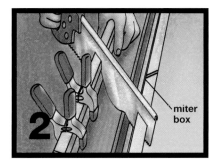

miter box

2 BEFORE PLACING the piece of molding in the miter box, support the molding on a scrap of lumber. This allows you to saw completely through the work without marring the bottom of the box. Place the molding against the far side of the miter box and make the cut with a backsaw. Hold the work firmly.

3 DRIVE THE HEADS of finishing nails below the surface with a hammer and nail set. Fill the hole with wood putty later.

4 FOR A PERFECTLY mitered look in corners, which are seldom perfectly square, run the first piece of crown molding tightly into the corner. Cope-cut the second piece of molding in the shape of the profile of the molding so it butts neatly against

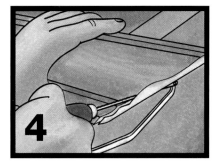

the face of the first piece.

5 THINK UPSIDE DOWN as you make miter cuts on crown molding. Place the face of the molding that goes against the ceiling on the bottom of the miter box. The bottom of the crown molding is the longest edge on inside corners. Use plenty of clamps to hold the molding to prevent it from moving while you cut it. Doing so helps ensure clean, accurate cuts.

6 CUT AWAY the excess wood along the back side of the molding with a coping saw.

carve away excess along coped cut

7 FINE-TUNE THE cut by using a utility knife to remove any excess material, but don't cut the exposed face of the molding. Test the fit. Take it down and carve it further, if necessary.

8 MAP OUT THE JOB so one end of each piece of molding is cut straight and one end is mitered and coped. Use butt joints if you have

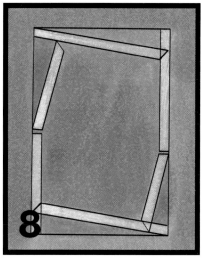

long runs of molding.

9 IF MOLDING RUNS perpendicular to ceiling joists, determine the location of the joists before you begin nailing the molding in place and nail into the joists. Drill pilot holes to keep the molding from splitting.

10 IF THE MOLDING runs parallel to the ceiling joists, cut a beveled face of 2×2, as shown, to length and screw it into the wall in the corner of the ceiling and the wall. The 2×2 provides a solid surface to which you can nail the molding, preventing the molding from sagging.

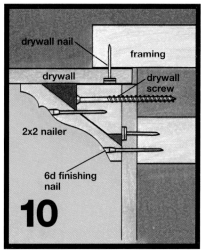

drywall nail

framing

drywall

drywall screw

2x2 nailer

6d finishing nail

index

CONTRIBUTORS/RESOURCES
Pages 43, 52–53: Crate & Barrell, all furniture and accessories; Jim Krantz and Kristsada/ Krantz Studio, photography.

Pages 53, 56: Dan Weeks, photography.